Cambridge Studies in French

MALLARMÉ, MANET AND REDON

T0381650

Cambridge Studies in French

General editor: MALCOLM BOWIE

1 Manet, *Portrait of Mallarmé*, 1876

2 Courbet, *Portrait of Baudelaire*, c. 1847

Mallarmé, Manet and Redon

VISUAL AND AURAL SIGNS AND
THE GENERATION OF MEANING

PENNY FLORENCE

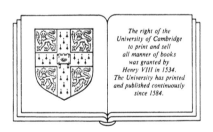

The right of the
University of Cambridge
to print and sell
all manner of books
was granted by
Henry VIII in 1534.
The University has printed
and published continuously
since 1584.

CAMBRIDGE UNIVERSITY PRESS

Cambridge
London   New York   New Rochelle
Melbourne   Sydney

CAMBRIDGE UNIVERSITY PRESS
Cambridge, New York, Melbourne, Madrid, Cape Town, Singapore, São Paulo, Delhi

Cambridge University Press
The Edinburgh Building, Cambridge CB2 8RU, UK

Published in the United States of America by Cambridge University Press, New York

www.cambridge.org
Information on this title: www.cambridge.org/9780521114585

First published 1986
This digitally printed version 2009

A catalogue record for this publication is available from the British Library

Library of Congress Cataloguing in Publication data
Florence, Penny
Mallarmé, Manet and Redon.
(Cambridge studies in French)
Bibliography: p.
Includes index.
1. Mallarmé, Stéphane, 1842–1898 – Criticism and
interpretation. 2. Manet, Edouard, 1832–1883.
3. Redon, Odilon, 1840–1916. 4. Art and literature – France.
5. Painting, Modern – 19th century – France. 6. Painting,
French. I. Title. II. Series.
PQ2344.Z5F48   1985   841′.8   85-9651

ISBN 978-0-521-30570-9 hardback
ISBN 978-0-521-11458-5 paperback

CONTENTS

ILLUSTRATIONS

PREFACE

Recent developments in criticism have begun to make it possible to articulate areas of cultural experience which were previously inaccessible or invisible. The precise nature of the relation between Mallarmé and painting is one such. Although it has long been recognised as a worthwhile and exciting subject it remains a gap in our knowledge of a period of dramatic change. Little of substance has been written about it, and no study has attempted to define it as a whole.

To try and understand the structures common to the Mallarmé text and visual expression reflects back on to many of the central preoccupations which underlie current reassessment of cultural production. From the 1870s onwards, poets and painters engaged with problems of form in response to a need to re-invent linguistic and visual modes capable of expressing and shaping social and individual experience. Their struggle is in itself relevant today, especially in the force-fields which connect semiotics, psychoanalysis, the history of art and feminism. Critical theory is still grappling with separate but overlapping categories while trying to liberate itself from others which are clearly redundant. For example, feminists have been working to excavate women's writing and painting from patriarchal obscurity and to establish how their rediscovery affects our analysis of culture. This has problematised many questions; of aesthetic value, hierarchies of form, and the textual significance of gender. In the period covered by this book the image of women and the idea of the female was foregrounded in the search for a new system of signs and in the probing of the creative process. It signifies an intuition of the malaise of which the suppression and exclusion of women and of the values and qualities projected on to them are one result. There is a complementary case to be made concerning race and cross-cultural relationships, one which I am not competent to make. But this study remains incomplete without it.

This book does not claim to deal with all these large matters either fully or even in some cases directly. But in its preliminary re-examination of Mallarmé as an innovator in Western poetic language and of the developments in the painting of his contemporaries, it is informed by them. I hope it has a contribution to make to the general debate as well as to the study of Mallarmé, especially as regards the practice of historical criticism.

ACKNOWLEDGEMENTS

This book has taken a long time to write and I am indebted to many people for their help. I should like to thank them all very warmly. Nicole Ward, Bob Jones and Alan Bowness guided me in different ways through the initial research for the thesis which forms the basis. Together with Tim Clarke, Nicole Ward and Bob Jones also encouraged me to develop it into what is now a very different book. I am especially grateful to Malcolm Bowie for his understanding and invaluable guidance throughout that transformation. Readers of his books, especially of *Mallarmé and the Art of Being Difficult*, will recognise the extent of my debt to him, even where my position differs. Rosemary Jackson gave me her love and support from the earliest days as well as her criticism of the text. Sara Perren and Geoff Wall read and commented on the manuscript. And my thanks go especially to my friends. Without them all I could not have written it. And thanks to Val Simpson for her typing skill and her enthusiasm for the work.

Finally, I am grateful to the trustees of the F. R. Leavis fund at York University for their grant towards travelling to see paintings in the U.S.A.

York, 1986

For my mother, Eileen Florence
And in memory of my father,
Cecil Florence

1

INTRODUCTION

Poétiser, par art plastique, moyen de prestiges directs, semble, sans intervention, le fait de l'ambience éveillant aux surfaces leur lumineux secret: ou la riche analyse, chastement pour la restaurer, de la vie, selon une alchimie, – mobilité et illusion.

Mallarmé. Preface to the catalogue of Berthe Morisot's posthumous exhibition, 1896.

But the first idea was not to shape the clouds
In imitation. The clouds preceded us.

Wallace Stevens. 'Notes towards a Supreme Fiction'.

Language floats at the vanishing-point
'incarnate' breathes the flourescent bulb
'primary' states the scarred grain of the floor
and on the ceiling in torn plaster laughs 'imago'

Adrienne Rich. 'To a Poet'.

I could write in colours or in wordless sounds.

Anja Meulenbelt. 'The Shame is Over'.

This book is about Mallarmé and visual signification in painting and in language. By constructing a series of relationships I have aimed to clarify what is basically visual in Mallarmé, how it functions in his theory and practice and to connect such verbal signs with painting. More particularly, I have sought a consistent set of terms within which the very broad range of innovations in poetry and painting during the last thirty years of the nineteenth century may be understood, bringing out some sense of the coherence of these concerns in Mallarmé's writing. Further, I have tried to indicate through these visual movements and structures the kind of simplicity into which Mallarmé's shifts and uncertainties can form.

There have been two basic barriers to carrying this out, and they are quite closely linked. It is not just that the initial facts are scattered, as they are, nor that two art forms and several media are involved. The problem stems from the way the history of what is known as 'the rise of modernism' has been constructed and the conflicting values and conceptual categories enshrined in the criteria we bring to understanding texts. This is of course one of the central problems addressed in post-structuralist approaches to language and communication, especially in the debates centred on the status of Literature and High Culture. The difficulty is acute when it comes to tracking 'the visual' in Mallarmé's textual world, more so perhaps for those of us working outwards from British traditions of art history and criticism.

Mallarmé's last poem, 'Un Coup de Dés' provides an acute instance of the problem. I have devoted my fourth chapter to reading it in conjunction with its proposed illustrations (figs. 59–61), and I refer to it at several points in the broader argument. It is hard enough to arrive at an adequate sense of how the poem's visual appearance functions in relation to its syntax or how active its typography and spaces are semantically. How then do we take account of its illustrations? The sense we mainly have of 'Un Coup de Dés' and of the modernist tradition into which it has been inserted does not readily accommodate even the idea that illustrations might be appropriate. Still less does this sense prepare us for the three lithographs which were made for it (four were planned). On the whole they have either been ignored or dismissed. They are by Odilon Redon, and are the last of his black and white lithographic series, the first of which was begun in 1879. Many of these lithographs were transpositions from literature – including the Bible and works by Poe, Flaubert, Goethe, Baudelaire, and Bulwer-Lytton – and they were highly regarded among artists in France and Belgium in the 1880s and 1890s. In form they are properly grotesque, that is, incorporating distortions, incongruities and combinations of human, animal and vegetable forms. The lithographs for 'Un Coup de Dés' are no exception. The poem would seem to be too complete, too modern and too abstract to allow them anything other than a very secondary, if not redundant, function. Quite apart from any aesthetic power the illustrations may or may not have, readers today may well resist opening the poem to them. And yet it, too, is discontinuous in its movements and meanings.

If we take as another example Manet's illustrations for Poe's 'The Raven', (figs. 22–27) with Mallarmé's prose translation, made in 1875, further troublesome factors seem to emerge, different from those raised by the Redon series. They appear, at first, untypical of Manet in medium and form, and their relation to the text is not simple. Nor is it nowadays immediately apparent how they relate Manet, as an Impressionist, to Poe and Mallarmé. Like the Redon, however, they are part of a larger pattern, one which gradually brings these two painters, Manet and Redon, and the different 'movements' they are supposed to belong to, into closer relation. At the time they were executed, Mallarmé wrote two substantial essays on Manet and Impressionism. In the second essay he outlined a programme which is, to my mind, very illuminating in its predictions for the later nineteenth century. Its coherence has since been obscured. Mallarmé's historical analysis, and the formal innovations which developed both at the time and subsequently, do in fact confirm each other. These historical and formal problems underlie the arguments and explorations in this book.

The second chapter, therefore, integrates Mallarmé's extensive essay of 1876, 'The Impressionists and Edouard Manet', into his theory of poetry. This contextualisation is focused on 'Crise de Vers', because there are similarities of internal structure between the two essays, which both attempt to assess the implications of a radical break with tradition and to make some tentative projection as to its future development. Mallarmé's analyses bring together important theoretical aspects of two separated traditions of the avant-garde: Impressionism and Symbolism. Manet's production stands in no clearer relation to high art and the traditions its enshrines than Redon's. In neither case, nor in Mallarmé's, is it enough to place them in opposition – to the received, to the official, to each other, to 'reality'. They all offer innovations which open on to enriching ways of making sense, provided their disruptive movements are understood as integral to their structure, and their power felt.

There is a very comfortable view of Impressionism according to which it is a technique for recording light, naturalism, an optic. In 'The Impressionists and Edouard Manet', Mallarmé takes Courbet as his starting point and attempts to construct an analysis of Manet which is capable, not of fusing all post-Romantic painting, but of understanding its variety according to common precepts. In his approach to understanding the assemblage of technical devices in Manet he also seeks out the interaction between the function of secondary patterns and experiential disjunctions. His analysis (written before the 1880s, pointillism, neo-Impressionism, the Nabis, the Salon de la Rose-et-Croix and all the rest) provides cues when complex and difficult texts such as 'Un Coup de Dés' signify by means of supposedly opposed functions. To record an altered perceptual fact such as perspective or the effect of light, initiates far-reaching changes in ways that affect not only visual experience. Novel experience and perception are not ineffable though they may be only glimpsed in parts, or through breaks in structure.

In the third chapter I have tried to understand and to describe the main innovations made by Mallarmé and his contemporaries in painting, how these innovations interrelate, working from the breadth and openness which characterise the framework of 'The Impressionists and Edouard Manet'. That essay itself shifts its levels of 'argument' in a highly stimulating manner, constantly opening out, proposing change and new directions. Like most of the texts in this study, it demands of the reader active participation in making meaning and coherence clear. The structures in these texts necessitate a theory of signs, initiating a self-conscious signifying practice. This chapter therefore is a description of semiotic practices common to poems and paintings, and an attempt to understand the semantics of form in them. Movement and change are basic to this exploration of form. I shall expand on this before going on to describe the fourth chapter.

Any sign-system may be modified to accommodate matter hitherto exclusive to another, in the same way as any language may be extended to express new concepts and feelings. Differences lie in what the system compels the sender to convey, not in what it allows. By the multiplication of signs, an exponential growth in meaning is possible and, at a different pace, greater freedom gained from what has to be said. Freedom, for example, from gender categorisation, from hierarchical, prescriptive forms which seek to inhibit change or to exclude or devalue areas of thought and experience; in short, from oppression. Texts which foreground their own creative process may be read, not as decadent 'art for art's sake', but as focusing the movements within the culture, its languages and sign-systems, and between cultures, in such a way as to articulate its distortions and exclusions.

The construction of historical categories, and the problematic status of certain forms within it, results in part from ascribing value or priority to signs which are either clearly visual or clearly aural.[1] So-called 'literary' painting, for example, tends to be described as less significant than purely 'visual' art. The same is true of explicitly philosophical and narrative art, both in poetry and painting. There follows a regularising process in which some features are erased or submerged. This normalisation has applied to partial readings of complex signs and what I call transmutative operations.[2] It can happen in a given text, in an author's production or in intertextual analysis.[3] It inhibits both understanding of form and psychological interpretation. But we are beginning to find ways of moving beyond these structural divisions between 'visual' and 'verbal' knowledge.

'Un Coup de Dés', for example, promotes an awareness of written language as a particular kind of complex signifier. Since written language is seen as well as capable of being heard, it has a visual and spatial element. Since one form, the icon,[4] predominates among visual and spatial signs, and another, the symbol,[5] among auditory and temporal signs, by combining them in a certain way, written language traverses different fields of semiotic potential. There is a temporal duality, a kind of 'time warp' involved in the crossover between systems, which may be evident in verbal or visual art. This is an essential part of language in its written form – and one which Mallarmé foregrounds – because the transmission of a linguistic message on a page introduces a spatial dimension and reduces the temporal. Analysing this fundamental relation between the iconic and the symbolic also provides a means of bringing together the separated avant-garde traditions, starting with Impressionism and Symbolism.

Mallarmé's exploitation of the division between visual and aural signs allows his language greater freedom as a transgressive form, activating both its written and its spoken potential. We are made aware of language as seen and as heard. Music comes into this deliberate restructuring, as metaphor, as perfect semiosis, as rhythm and song. This dimension of nineteenth-century aesthetics is symptomatic of the development of new emotive potential in the text. The quality of feeling generated is no less extraordinary and mobile than the novelty of structure and is a function of it. But rather than *identifying* music with the non-representational or affective in art, it

may be understood as integral to its complex transmutative character. It is
introversive, which has two main effects: by referring to itself it draws attention to
the workings of the code and the message itself; and by its subjectivity it involves
both sender and receiver of the message. All parts of message-transmission are
thereby activated. It is in this sense that I understand certain main references to
music in Mallarmé, such as the following from 'Quant au Livre':

L'écrit, envol tacite d'abstraction, reprend ses droits en face de la chute des sons nus; tous deux,
Musique et lui, intimant une préalable disjonction, celle de la parole, certainement par effroi de fournir
au bavardage.
Même aventure contradictoire, où ceci descend; dont s'évade cela; mais non sans traîner les gazes
d'origine.   (385)[6]

As Merleau-Ponty said of Cézanne,[7] it is not a matter of choosing between
thought and feeling, order and chaos, or of departing from the phenomenal world
instead of imitating it. Rather it is the depiction of both the stable things we see and
the shifting ways in which they appear – 'appear' being active and reciprocal, process
and emergence. It is a 'lived perspective' which 'summons one away from the already
constituted reason in which "cultured men" are content to shut themselves, towards
a reason which contains its own origins'.

What we have come to know as 'pure' poetry and pure painting are in fact shifting
and multiple. For example, Redon's signifying practice involves a clear movement
between visual and aural sign-systems, since he combines words and pictures. The
image of his lithographic series, whether these comprise illustrations or independent
albums, establishes a variable relation, internally between its component parts, and
externally with other images in the series and in relation to the caption or titles – the
verbal component. This is the basis for constructing an exact but fluid and complex
new signified. A similarly mobile structure, but without words, exists in Manet.
His paintings may be seen to work in a combination of ways which generate meaning
out of a syntactic structure in the manner of an aural sign. To varying degrees of
complexity, this principle applies to Mallarmé and to the painters in this study who
worked towards making new meanings, using visual and aural structures in
combination. They all moved towards the perfect sign, which is not unitary or
exclusively introversive,[8] but is a transition. It does not convey an ideal or a perfect
image of something, but it makes innovation possible by incorporating movement
and time.

In these texts, then, there is a breakdown of structures which hierarchise, or
which are built on the assumption that the truth is accessible as an isolate. They
reject and attack the notion of the 'real' as unitary in representation. They indicate
how formal innovation in visual art and language qualify each other in cognitive and
semiotic terms.

In several ways, the visual may come before the verbal in epistemology and in
semiotic structures, as for example in the restricted senses that most people see
before they can speak, and that when reading, the first impression of a text is visual.

Thus, since the process of innovation involves a return to beginnings, the question of how 'the visual' works is insistently posed in these texts. Seeking to define the specific function of the visual in initiating new meanings is not simple, however. 'Seeing' does not remain on the level of perception, as is implied in many accounts of Impressionism. When we see differently, both verbal consciousness and the verbal in relation to consciousness are affected. Understanding how articulation and consciousness interact is a necessary first step to understanding what this implies both for art practice, and for interpretation; because understanding what works mean in the present seems to me a vital part of practice. When, as in these texts, meanings become unstable and mercurial, we need to know what makes them precise, and where they are clear in meaning, not just to seek one set of meanings, as a true and permanent system, closed and exclusive. Since these texts make no distinction between form and content, meaning will change through extrinsic factors in conjunction with internal structural movements. This is a kind of poise, close to the perfect sign, anterior to systematisation; it may be characterised as either transmutative or syncretic. In trying to describe these functions I have drawn on linguistic and psychoanalytic theory[9] to structure my subjective responses to the texts, to take account of time, and to develop a sense of that movement (or regression) to primary process (or unmediated experience) which the perfect sign reaches toward. By regression I do not mean dissolution, or some notion of unmarked precultural modes to which a return may be made. I mean the incorporation into the text of mental and perceptual processes which are neither logically nor linguistically organised, forming a texture in which the rational and the communicable are embedded. The texts involve a kind of formalism, but seen as a function in the social and political conditions of its production. What is communicable in art, either as information or as aesthetic power, is in constant interchange with recorded structures of thought and with perceptual knowledge in all forms.

In my third chapter, which is about form and meaning, I approach the intertextuality of poems and paintings through a structural analysis because in this way it should be possible to write about meaning without perpetuating the 'form-and-content' division which is an obstacle to reading texts whose formal interrogation of meaning is of equal weight to their tentative deposition of it. 'Deposition': taking down, dethroning, but also a process of depositing, a testimony or statement, an inversion of meaning which is common in the texts under discussion. Linguistic or semiotic inversion involves no simple antithesis, because the connoted meanings of a word in its contradictory uses – latent and contextual in the sense that they apply only when inserted into an unambiguous framework – are not in themselves simply oppositions. By maintaining variable meanings of the word in context, a whole series of possibilities is introduced. These are not associative in the looser sense, but depend on how the sentence is constructed overall. Meaning is thus generated through further opposition – that of structure and connotation. If we call the first internal, because it is unique in every instance, and the second external, because it is not, then we can describe this way of generating meaning in terms which may be applied to transmutative structural functions in general. That is, to any written or painted text which reaches out beyond its initiating structure and meaning – which innovates. In so doing, the text will compel attention to its own insufficiency, and inscribe both the possibility always of saying more – because it has said more than was possible before it existed – and never enough – because by opening up a code, [10] the text leaves its reminder that it is incomplete. This generates excitement, but also unpleasure, like Freud's unbound cathexes. [11] The infinity of desire is inscribed, to put it in Lacanian terms.

This is a process of initiating meanings which has been interpreted as belonging to so-called primitive thought processes. Its reintroduction into rationally organised, highly developed systems of meaning is strange in its effect. The present form of the language, and those who experience it as sender or receiver, are made to incorporate the past at both subjective and cultural levels. Writing inaugurates; but not *ex nihilo*. This embodiment of the past is a denial of linear time. It is experienced as a shock, both in the particular instance and in its repercussions. Again, a simple extension from the individual to the cultural, or in Freudian terms, from the ontogenetic to the phylogenetic cannot legitimately be made, especially if it results in universalising. But it cannot be avoided altogether, if we are to see why Western culture produced such a diversity of forms – a Redon and a Monet, a Manet and a Moreau, for example – at the same time; and, furthermore, why these forms seemed consistent to a Mallarmé, yet remained irreconcilable to most of his contemporaries and critical inheritors.

The fifth chapter returns to some dominant nineteenth-century myths and images, and relates them to gender and to the Oedipal moment. In so doing it approaches what is a general problem for any avant-garde, and for any art which is active in social change. How does it convey the positive values towards which it reaches, when it has to oppose and to negate? The difficulty is compounded by the need to move beyond the oppositional to that position where new meanings may begin to change to determining structure. This is one of the tasks feminism has taken on, a task to which these texts have much to contribute. My emphasis is not on specific images of woman, and a great deal more could be said about how such images associate the female with for example, the occult, or the spiritual ideal or the uncanny or the threatening; that is, with a series of abstractions on the margins or extremes of experience. Mallarmé texts such as *La Dernière Mode*, or his translated tales, may be read as radical in their exploration of modes conventionally gendered female. Less accessibly, the same is true of his formal and linguistic experimentation, leading to the limits of language and form at an experiential level, their interaction with reality and their capacity either to construct or convey. Among the reasons why this connection is not easy to make, formal and historical obstacles such as those explored in Mallarmé's critical texts in chapter two re-emerge, and in closer focus. The difficulty of establishing what we mean by, for example, the abstract is a part of the general imprecision in our critical apparatus, our confusions between representation, semiosis, mimesis and so forth, and the inadequacy of these terms to describe how the varying tropes shift. Does 'abstract' mean non-objective, in Arp's sense of images which represent nothing else, or in Mondrian's sense of an image refined out of its subject? How do these distinctions relate to the supposed perceptual base of Cubism, or to the conjunction of abstract and representational form in, say, Klee?

What is at issue here is both conceptions of reality and relations of the individual reader and of the text to the signifying process, to the status of the visual, as sign and as experience. Lacan, for example, in his writing on the scopic[12] and other partly derivative instinctual drives, proposes that the visual has a primary and initiating function, that it establishes fundamental patterns at the genesis of culture; and also that it is constructed as male. This series of manoeuvres conflates terms, one of which may then be given *a priori* status. It then appears to determine the rest, to become an absolute.

For example, if connoted meanings are allowed as structural rather than secondary this exposure and reassigning of value begins to break down the barriers which exclude women and the otherwise dispossessed as makers of meaning. Gender definition is one instance of an implicit merging of the cultural and biological, endowing the power of the one with the permanence of the other. Poetic metaphors of creativity and birth are imbricated with each other, and are open to this kind of appropriation to confirm the immutability of received meanings.

In Mallarmé there is a sense of broken lineage, especially strong after the death of his son, Anatole. This ontological crisis informs the cyclic and ritual movements of his poems – the sun's course, the seasons, the heroic journey, the burial. Crisis is also signified by those details and objects which at first seem a distraction; like the syntactic breaks they begin to signify and then, in the same moment, deflect. This is a movement which itself signifies; and through it there appears a way to reshape the past-in-language. Gender traverses these shifts at new points where distinctions need to be made. Wendy Mulford writes that we cannot assume that work for a text such as 'Un Coup de Dés' was produced from a differently gendered place.[13] She describes as colonial the relation that women have to historically significant texts within a culture and language in which women are not at ease. 'Un Coup de Dés' is, however, a text which resists being placed in that culture, while remaining impossible to ignore. There is no feeling at ease with 'Un Coup de Dés' or with the 'modernist' tradition. They were produced out of dis-ease. How we relate to this dis-ease is a problem shared by all writing subjects. It is not, however, the same shape irrespective of gender:

legs en la disparition

à quelqu'un

ambigu   ('Un Coup de Dés', 464)

To understand the visual in Mallarmé and how it relates to the painting of his contemporaries is also to address these questions. The texts show a concern with dislocated individualism and social structures. They attempt to gain freedom from restrictive cultural accretions, but without total loss in the production of the new. From the present perspective, the question of gender is integral to reading their redefinition of tradition. It is a necessary part of the process of clarifying how accounts of nineteenth-century art have been partial and often falsified.

2

A NEW PROBLEMATIC OF THE IMAGINARY

And here occurs one of those unexpected crises which appear in art. Let us study it in its present condition and its future prospects and with some attempt to develop its idea.

'The Impressionists and Edouard Manet'.

La Littérature ici subit une exquise crise, fondamentale.

Qui accorde à cette fonction une place où la première, reconnaît, là, la fait de l'actualité: on assiste, comme finale d'un siècle, pas ainsi que ce fut dans le dernier, à des bouleversements; mais hors de la place publique, à une inquiétude du voile dans le temple avec des plis significatifs et un peu sa dechirure.

'Crise de Vers'

Le passé compris de sa race qui pèse sur lui en la sensation de fini, l'heure de la pendule précipitant cet ennui en temps lourd, étouffant, et son attente de l'accomplissement du futur, forment du temps pur, ou de l'ennui, rendu instable par la maladie de l'idéalité: cet ennui, ne pouvant être, redevient ses éléments, tantôt, tous les meubles fermés, et pleins de leur secret;...

'Igitur'

Silence, excepté que paraît un spectacle d'enchantement moderne. Loin, ou dès la croisée qui prépare à l'exterieur et maintient, dans une attente verte d'Hespérides aux simples oranges et parmi la brique rose d'Eldorados, tout à coup l'irruption à quelque carafe, éblouissamment du jour, tandis que multicolore il se propage en perses et en tapis rejouis, le génie, distillateur de la Crise, où cesse l'étincelle des chimères au mobilier, est, d'abord, d'un peintre.

Preface to Berthe Morisot posthumous exhibition.

'The Impressionists and Edouard Manet'

What follows is the complete text of Mallarmé's article, published in English under the above title. The translation appeared in *The Art Monthly Review* (September 1876, the month after W. M. Rossetti's 'Pre-Raphaelitism, its starting-point and its sequel'). It was approved by Mallarmé after corrections.[1] The original in French appears to have been lost. The article was only easily available in an incomplete retranslation in French until 1968,[2] and it remains comparatively unknown.[3] Like its less ambitious predecessor, 'Le Jury de Peinture pour 1874 et M. Manet', the article was intended to support Manet in his attempt to gain recognition from the official *Salon*, but its scope is far broader. It is a fascinating and acute assessment of developments in painting in the 1870s and of their implications.

'The Impressionists and Edouard Manet'

3   Manet, *Le Linge*, 1876

Without any preamble whatsoever, without even a word of explanation to the reader who may be ignorant of the meaning of the title which heads this article, I shall enter at once into its subject, reserving to myself either to draw my deductions, new from an art point of view, as the facts I relate present themselves or leave them to ooze out when and as they may.

Briefly, then, let us take a short glimpse backward on art history. Rarely do our annual exhibitions abound with novelty, and some few years back such years of abundance were still more rare; but about 1860 a sudden and a lasting light shone forth when Courbet (figs. 2 and 4) began to exhibit his works. These then in some degree coincided with that movement which had appeared in literature, and which obtained the name of Realism; that is to say, it sought to impress itself upon the mind by the lively depiction of things as they appeared to be, and vigorously excluded all meddlesome imagination. It was a great movement, equal in intensity to that of the Romantic school, just then expiring under the hands of the landscape painters, or to that later one whence issued the bold decorative effects of Henri Regnault (fig. 5); and it then moved on many a new and contemporaneous path. But in the midst of this, there began to appear, sometimes perchance on the walls of the Salon, but far more frequently and certainly on those of the galleries of the rejected, curious and singular paintings – laughable to the many, it is true, from their very faults, but nevertheless very disquieting to the true and reflective critic, who could not refrain from asking himself what manner of man is this? and what the strange doctrine he preaches? For it was evident that the preacher had a meaning; he was persistent in his reiteration, unique in his persistency, and his works were signed by the then new and unknown name of EDOUARD MANET. There was also at that time, alas! that it should have to be written in the past tense, an enlightened amateur, one who loved all arts and lived for one of them. These strange pictures at once won his sympathy; an instinctive and poetic foresight made him love them; and this before their prompt succession and the sufficient exposition of the principles they inculcated had revealed their meaning to the thoughtful few of the public many. But this enlightened amateur died too soon to see these, and before his favourite painter had won a public name.

That amateur was our last poet, Charles Baudelaire (fig. 2).

Following in appreciative turn came the then coming novelist Emile Zola. With that insight into the future which distinguishes his own works, he recognized the light that had arisen, albeit that he was yet too young to then define that which we to-day call Naturalism, to follow the quest, not merely of that reality which impresses itself in its abstract form on all, but of that absolute and important sentiment which Nature herself impresses on those who have voluntarily abandoned conventionalism.

In 1867 a special exhibition of the works of Manet and some few of his followers, gave to the then nameless school of recent painting which thus grew up, the semblance of a party, and party strife grew high. The struggle with this resolute intruder was preached as a crusade from the rostrum of each school. For several years a firm and implacable front was formed against its advance; until at length vanquished by its good faith and persistency, the jury recognised the name of Manet, welcomed it, and so far recovered from its ridiculous fears, that it reasoned and found it must either declare him a self-created sovereign pontiff, charged by his own faith with the cure of souls, or condemn him as a heretic and a public danger.

The latter of these alternatives being now-a-days definitively adopted, the public exhibition of Manet's works has of late taken place in his own studio. Yet, and notwithstanding all this, and in spite of concurrent Salons, the public rushed with lively curiosity and eagerness to the Boulevard des Italiens and the galleries of Durand Ruel in 1874 and 1876, to see the works of those then styled the Intransigeants, now the Impressionists. And what found they there? A collection of pictures of strange aspect, at first view giving the ordinary impression of the motive which made them, but over beyond this, a peculiar quality outside mere Realism. And here occurs one of those unexpected crises which appear in art. Let us study it in its present condition and its future prospects, and with some attempt to develop its idea.

Manet, when he casts away the cares of art and chats with a friend between the lights in his studio, expresses himself with brilliancy. Then it is that he tells him what he means by Painting; what new destinies are yet in store for it; what it is, and how that it is from an irrepressible instinct that he paints, and that he paints as he does. Each time he begins a picture, says he, he plunges headlong into it, and feels like a man who knows that his surest plan to learn to swim safely is, dangerous as it may seem, to throw himself into the water. One of his habitual aphorisms then is that no one should paint a landscape and a figure by the same process, with the same knowledge, or in the same fashion; nor what is more, even two landscapes or two figures. Each work should be a new creation of the mind. The hand, it is true, will conserve some of its acquired secrets of manipulation, but the eye should forget all else it has seen, and learn anew from the lesson before it. It should abstract itself from memory, seeing only that which it looks upon, and that as for the the first time; and the hand should become an impersonal abstraction guided only by the will, oblivious of all previous cunning. As for the artist himself, his personal feeling, his peculiar tastes, are for the time absorbed, ignored, or set aside for the enjoyment of his personal life. Such a result as this cannot be attained all at once. To reach it the master must pass through many phases ere this self-isolation can be acquired, and this new evolution of art be learnt; and I, who have occupied myself a good deal in its study, can count but two who have gained it.

Wearied by the technicalities of the school in which, under Couture, he studied, Manet, when he recognised the inanity of all he was taught, determined either not to paint at all or to paint entirely from without himself. Yet, in his self-sought insulation, two masters – masters of the past – appeared to him, and befriended him in his revolt. Velasquez, and the painters of the Flemish school, particularly impressed themselves upon him, and the wonderful atmosphere·which enshrouds the compositions of the grand old Spaniard, and the brilliant tones which glow from the canvasses of his northern compeers, won the student's admiration, thus presenting to him two art aspects which he has since made himself the master of, and can mingle as he pleases. It is precisely these two aspects which reveal the truth, and give paintings based upon them living reality instead of rendering them the baseless fabric of abstracted and obscure dreams. These have been the tentatives of Manet, and curiously, it was to the foreigner and the past that he turned for friendly council in remedying the evils of his country and his time. And yet truth bids me say that Manet had no pressing need for this; an incomparable copyist, he could have found his game close to hand had he chosen his quarry there; but he sought something more than this, and fresh things are not found all at once; freshness, indeed, frequently consists – and this is especially the case in these critical days – in a co-ordination of widely-scattered elements.

The pictures in which this reve:sion to the traditions of the old masters of the north and south are found constitute Manet's first manner. Now the old writers on art expressed by the word 'manner,' rather the lavish blossoming of genius during one of its intellectual seasons than the fact fathered, found, or sought out by the painter himself. But that in which the painter declares most his views is the choice of his subjects. Literature often departs from its current path to seek for the aspirations of an epoch of the past, and to modernise them for its own purpose, and in painting Manet followed a similarly divergent course, seeking the truth, and loving it when found, because being true it was so strange, especially when compared with old and worn-out ideals of it. Welcomed on his outset, as we have said, by Baudelaire, Manet fell under the influence of the moment, and, to illustrate him at this period, let us take one of his first works, 'Olympia' (fig 71); that wan, wasteld courtesan, showing to the public, for the first time, the non-traditional, unconventional nude. The bouquet, yet enclosed in its paper envelope, the gloomy cat (apparently suggested by one of the prose poems of the author of the 'Fleurs du Mal,') and all the surrounding accessories, were truthful, but not immoral – that is, in the ordinary and foolish sense of the word – but they were undoubtedly intellectually perverse in their tendency. Rarely has any modern work been more applauded by some few, or more deeply damned by the many, than was that of this innovator.

If our humble opinion can have any influence in this impartial history of the work of the chief of the new school of painting, I would say that the transition period in it is by no means to be regretted. Its parallel is found in literature, when our sympathies are suddenly awakened by some new imagery presented to us; and this is what I like in Manet's work. It surprised us all as something long hidden but suddenly revealed. Captivating and repulsive at the same time, eccentric, and new, such types as he gave us were needed in our ambient life. In them, strange though they were, there was nothing vague, general, conventional, or hackneyed. Often they attracted attention by something peculiar in the physiognomy of his subject, half hiding or sacrificing to those new laws of space and light he set himself to inculcate, some minor details which others would have seized upon.

Bye and bye, if he continues to paint long enough, and to educate the public eye – as yet veiled by conventionality – if that public will then consent to see the true beauties of the people, healthy and solid as they are, the graces which exist in the bourgeoisie will then be recognised and taken as worthy models in art, and then will come the time of peace. As yet it is but one of struggle – a struggle to render those truths in nature which for her are eternal, but which are as yet for the multitude but new.

The reproach which superficial people formulate against Manet, that whereas once he painted ugliness now he paints vulgarity, falls harmlessly to the ground, when we recognise the fact that he paints the truth, and recollect those difficulties he encountered on his way to seek it, and how he conquered them. *Un Déjeuner sur l'Herbe, L'Exécution de Maximilien, Un Coin de Table, Des Gens du monde à la Fenêtre, Le Bon Bock, Un Coin de Bal de l'Opéra, Le Chemin de Fer*, and the two *Canotiers* (figs. 8–14, 16)[4] – these are the pictures which step by step have marked each round in the ladder scaled by this bold innovator, and which have led him to the point achieved in his truly marvellous work, this year refused by the Salon, but exhibited to the public by itself, entitled *Le Linge* (fig. 3) – a work which marks a date in a life-time perhaps, but certainly one in the history of art.

The whole of the series we have just above enumerated with here and there an exception, demonstrate the painter's aim very exactly; and this aim was not to make a momentary escapade or sensation, but by steadily endeavouring to impress upon his work a natural and a general law, to seek out a type rather than a personality, and to flood it with light and air; and such air! air which despotically dominates over all else. And before attempting to analyse this celebrated picture I should like to comment somewhat on that truism of to-morrow, that paradox of to-day, which in studio slang is called 'the theory of open air' or at least on that which it becomes with the authoritative evidence of the later efforts of Manet. But here is first of all an objection to overcome. Why is it needful to represent the open air of gardens, shore or street, when it must be owned that the chief part of modern existence is passed within doors? There are many answers; among these I hold the first, that in the atmosphere of any interior, bare or furnished, the reflected lights are mixed and broken and too often discolour the flesh tints. For instance I would remind you of a painting in the salon of 1873 which our painter justly called a *Rêverie*.[5] There a young woman reclines on a divan exhaling all the lassitude of summer time; the jalousies of her room are almost closed, the dreamer's face is dim with shadow, but a vague, deadened daylight suffuses her figure and her muslin dress. This work is altogether exceptional and sympathetic.

Woman is by our civilisation consecrated to night, unless she escape from it sometimes to those open air afternoons by the seaside or in an arbour, affectionated by moderns. Yet I think the artist would be in the wrong to present her among the artificial glories of candle-light or gas, as at that time the only object of art would be the woman herself, set off by the immediate atmosphere, theatrical and active, even beautiful, but utterly inartistic. Those persons much accustomed, whether from the habit of their calling or purely from taste, to fix on a mental canvas the beautiful remembrance of woman, even when thus seen amid the glare of night in the world or at the theatre, must have remarked that some mysterious process despoils the noble phantom of the artificial prestige cast by candelabra or footlights, before she is admitted fresh and simple to the number of every day haunters of the imagination. (Yet I must own that but few of those whom I have consulted on this obscure and delicate point are of my opinion.) The complexion, the special beauty which springs from the very source of life, changes with artificial lights, and it is probably from the desire to preserve this grace in all its integrity, that painting – which concerns itself more about this flesh-pollen than any other human attraction – insists on the mental operation to which I have lately alluded, and demands daylight – that is space with the transparence of air alone. The natural light of day penetrating into and influencing all things, although itself invisible, reigns also on this typical picture called *The Linen*, which we will study next, it being a complete and final repertory of all current ideas and the means of their execution.

Some fresh but even-coloured foliage – that of a town garden – holds imprisoned a flood of summer morning air. Here a young woman, dressed in blue, washes some linen, several pieces of which are already drying; a child coming out from the flowers looks at its mother – that is all the subject. This picture is life-size, though this scale is somewhat lower in the middle distance, the painter wisely recognising the artificial requirements forced upon him by the arbitrarily fixed point of view imposed on the spectator. It is deluged with air. Everywhere the luminous and transparent atmosphere struggles with the figures, the dresses, and the foliage, and seems to take to itself some of their substance and solidity; whilst their contours, consumed by the hidden sun and wasted by space, tremble, melt, and evaporate into the surrounding atmosphere, which plunders reality from the figures, yet seems to do so in order to preserve their truthful aspect. Air reigns supreme and real, as if it held an enchanted life conferred by the witchery of art; a life neither personal nor sentient, but itself subjected to the phenomena thus called up by the science and shown to our astonished eyes, with its perpetual metamorphosis and its invisible action rendered visible. And how? By this fusion or by this struggle ever continued between surface and space, between colour and air. Open air: – that is the beginning and end of the question we are now studying. Aesthetically it is answered by the simple fact that there in open air alone can the flesh tints of a model keep their true qualities, being nearly equally lighted on all sides. On the other hand if one paints the real or artificial half-light in use in the schools, it is this feature or that feature on which the light strikes and forces into undue relief, according to an easy means for a painter to dispose a face to suit his own fancy and return to by-gone styles.

The search after truth, peculiar to modern artists, which enables them to see nature and reproduce her, such as she appears to just and pure eyes, must lead them to adopt air almost exclusively as their medium, or at all events to habituate themselves to work in it freely and without restraint: there should at least be in the revival of such a medium, if nothing more, an incentive to a new manner of painting. This is the result of our reasoning, and the end I wish to establish. As no artist has on his palette a transparent and neutral colour answering to open air, the desired effect can only be obtained by lightness or heaviness of touch, or by the regulation of tone. Now Manet and his school use simple colour, fresh, or lightly laid on, and their results appear to have been attained at the first stoke, that the ever-present light blends with and vivifies all things. As to the details of the picture, nothing should be absolutely fixed in order that we may feel that the bright gleam which lights the picture, or the diaphanous shadow which veils it, are only seen in passing, and just when the spectator beholds the represented subject, which being composed of a harmony of reflected and ever-changing lights, cannot be supposed always to look the same, but palpitates with movement, light, and life.

But will not this atmosphere – which an artifice of the painter extends over the whole of the object painted – vanish, when the completely finished work is as a repainted picture? If we could find no other way to indicate the presence of air than the partial or repeated application of colour as usually employed, doubtless the representation would be as fleeting as the effect represented, but from the first conception of the work, the space intended to contain the atmosphere has been indicated, so that when this is filled by the represented air, it is as unchangeable as the other parts of the picture. Then composition (to borrow once more the slang of the studio) must play a considerable part in the aesthetics of a master of the Impressionists? No; certainly not; as a rule the grouping of modern persons does not suggest it, and for this reason our painter is pleased to dispense with it, and at the same time to avoid both affectation and style. Nevertheless he must find something on which to establish his picture, though it be but for a minute – for the one thing needful is the time required by the spectator to see and admire the representation with that promptitude which just suffices for the connection of its truth. If we turn to natural perspective (not that utterly and artificially classic science which makes our eyes the dupes of a civilized education, but rather that artistic perspective which we learn from the extreme East – Japan for example) – and look at the sea-pieces of Manet, where the water at the horizon rises to the height of the frame, which alone interrupts it, we feel a new delight at the recovery of a long obliterated truth.

The secret of this is found in an absolutely new science, and in the manner of cutting down the pictures, and which gives to the frame all the charm of a merely fanciful boundary, such as that which is embraced at one glance of a scene framed in by the hands, or at least all of it found worthy to preserve. This is the picture, and the function of the frame is to isolate it; though I am aware that this is running counter to prejudice. For instance, what need is there to represent this arm, this hat, or that river bank, if they belong to someone or something exterior to the picture; the one thing to be attained is that the spectator accustomed among a crowd or in nature to isolate one bit which pleases him, though at the same time incapable of entirely forgetting the adjured details which unite the part to the whole, shall not miss in the work of art one of his habitual enjoyments, and whilst recognizing that he is before a painting half believes he sees the mirage of some natural scene. Some will probably object that all of these means have been more or less employed in the past, that dexterity – though not pushed so far – of cutting the canvass off so as to produce an illusion – perspective almost conforming to the exotic usage of barbarians – the light touch and fresh tones uniform and equal, or variously trembling with shifting lights – all these ruses and expedients in art have been found more than once in the English school, and elsewhere. But the assemblage for the first time of all these relative processes for an end, visible and suitable to the artistic expression of the needs of our times, this is no inconsiderable achievement in the cause of art, especially since a mighty will has pushed these means to their uttermost limits.

But the chief charm and true characteristic of one of the most singular men of the age is, that Manet (who is a visitor to the principal galleries both French and foreign, and an erudite student of painting) seems to ignore all that has been done in art by others, and draws from his own inner consciousness all his effects of simplification, the whole revealed by effects of light incontestably novel. This is the supreme originality of a painter by whom originality is doubly forsworn, who seeks to lose his personality in nature herself, or in the gaze of a multitude until then ignorant of her charms.

Without making a catalogue of the already very considerable number of Manet's works, it has been necessary to mark the successive order of his pictures, each one of them an exponent of some different effort, yet all connected by the self-same theory; valuable also as illustrating the career of the head of the school of Impressionists, or rather the initiator of the only effective movement in this direction; and as showing how he has patiently mastered the idea of which he is at present in full possession. The absence of all personal obtrusion in the manner of this painter's interpretation of nature, permits the critic to dwell so long as he pleases on his pictures without appearing to be too exclusively occupied by one man; yet we must be careful to remember that each work of a genius, singular because he abjures singularity, is an artistic production, unique of its kind, recognisable at first sight among all the schools of all ages. And can such a painter have pupils? Yes, and worthy ones; notably Mademoiselle Eva Gonzales, who to a just understanding of the master's stand-point unites qualities of youthfulness and grace all her own.

But his influence as from friend to friend is wider spread than that which the master exercises over the pupil, and sways all the painters of the day; for even the manner of those artists most strongly opposed in idea to his theory is in some degree determined by his practice. There is indeed no painter of consequence who during the last few years has not adopted or pondered over some one of the theories advanced by the Impressionists, and notably that of the open air, which influences all modern artistic thought. Some come near us and remain our neighbours; others, like M. Fantin-Latour and the late M. Chintreuil, painters without any common point of resemblance, while working out their own ideas have little by little attained to results often analogous to those of the Impressionists, thus creating between his school and that of academic painting a healthy, evident, true, and conjunctive branch of art, at present upheld even by the generality of art lovers. But the Impressionists themselves, those whom cosy studio chats and an amicable interchange of idea have enabled to push together towards new and unexpected horizons, and fresh-formed truths, such as MM. Claude Monet, Sisley and Pizzaro, paint wondrously alike; indeed a rather superficial observer at a pure and simple exhibition of Impressionism would take all their works to be those of one man – and that man, Manet. Rarely have three workers wrought so much alike, and the reason of the similitude is simple enough, for they each endeavour to suppress individuality for the benefit of nature. Nevertheless the visitor would proceed from this first impression, which is quite right as a synthesis, to perceiving that each artist has some favourite piece of execution analogous to the subject accepted rather than chosen by him, and this acceptation fostered by reason of the country of his birth or residence, for these artists as a rule find their subjects close to home, within an easy walk, or in their own gardens.

Claude Monet loves water, and it is his especial gift to portray its mobility and transparency, be it sea or river, grey and monotonous, or coloured by the sky. I have never seen a boat poised more lightly on the water than in his pictures, or a veil more mobile and light than his moving atmosphere. It is in truth a marvel. Sisley seizes the passing moments of the day; watches a fugitive cloud and seems to paint it in its flight; on his canvass the live air moves and the leaves yet thrill and tremble. He loves best to paint them in spring, 'when the young leves on the lyte wode, waxen al with wille,' or when red and gold and russet-green the last few fall in autumn; for then space and light are one, and the breeze stirring the foliage prevents it from becoming an opaque mass, too heavy for such an impression of mobility and life. On the other hand, Pizzaro, the eldest of the three, loves the thick shade of summer woods and the green earth, and does not fear the solidity which sometimes serves to render the atmosphere visible as a luminous haze saturated with sunlight. It is not rare for one of these three to steal a march on Manet, who suddenly perceiving their anticipated or explained tendency, sums up all their ideas in one powerful and masterly work. For them, rather are the subtle and delicate changes of nature, the many variations undergone in some long morning or afternoon by a thicket of trees on the water's side.

The most successful work of these three painters is distinguished by a sure yet wonderfully rapid execution. Unfortunately the picture buyer, though intelligent enough to perceive in these transcripts from nature much more than a mere revel of execution, since in these instantaneous and voluntary pictures all is harmonious, and were spoiled by a touch more or less, is the dupe of this real or apparent promptitude of labour, and though he pays for these paintings a price a thousand times inferior to their real value, yet is disturbed by the after-thought that such light productions might be multiplied *ad infinitum*; a merely commercial misunderstanding from which, doubtless, these artists will have still to suffer. Manet has been more fortunate, and receives an adequate price for his work. As thorough Impressionists, these painters (excepting M. Claude Monet, who treats it superbly) do not usually attempt the natural size of their subjects, neither do they take them from scenes of private life, but are before everything landscape painters, and restrict their pictures to that size easiest to look at, and with shut eye preserve the remembrance of.

With these, some other artists, whose originality has distanced them from other contemporary painters, frequently, and as a rule, exhibit their paintings, and share in most of the art theories I have reviewed here. These are Degas, Mademoiselle Berthe Morizot, (now Madame Eugène Manet,) and Renoir, to whom I should like to join Whistler, who is so well appreciated in France, both by critics and the world of amateurs, had he not chosen England as a field of his success.

The muslin drapery that forms a luminous, ever-moving atmosphere round the semi-nakedness of the young ballet-dancers; the bold, yet profoundly complicated attitudes of these creatures, thus accomplishing one of the at once natural and yet modern functions of women, have enchanted M. Degas, who can, nevertheless, be as delighted with the charms of those little washerwomen, who fresh and fair, though poverty-stricken, and clad but in camisole and petticoat, bend their slender bodies at the hour of work. No voluptuousness there, no sentimentality here; the wise and intuitive artist does not care to explore the trite and hackneyed view of his subject. A master of drawing, he has sought delicate lines and movements exquisite or grotesque, and of a strange new beauty, if I dare employ towards his works an abstract term, which he himself will never employ in his daily conversation.

More given to render, and very succinctly, the aspect of things, but with a new charm infused into it by feminine vision, Mademoiselle Berthe Morizot seizes the wonderfully the familiar presence of a woman of the world, or a child in the pure atmosphere of the sea-shore, or green lawn. Here a charming couple enjoy all the limpidity of hours where elegance has become artless; and there how pure an atmosphere veils this woman standing out of doors, or that one who reclines under the shade of an umbrella thrown among the grasses and frail flowers which a little girl in a clean dress is busy gathering. The airy foreground, even the furthermost outlines of sea and sky, have the perfection of an actual vision, and that couple yonder, the least details of whose pose is so well painted that one could recognise them by that alone, even if their faces, seen under the shady straw hats, did not prove them to be portrait sketches, give their own characteristics to the place they enliven by their visit. The air of preoccupation, of mundane care or secret sorrows, so generally characteristic of the modern artist's sketches from contemporary life, were never more notably absent than here; one feels that the graceful lady and child are in perfect ignorance that the pose unconsciously adopted to gratify an innate sense of beauty is perpetuated in this charming water-colour.

The shifting shimmer of gleam and shadow which the changing reflected lights, themselves influenced by every neighbouring thing, cast upon each advancing or departing figure, and the fleeting combinations in which these dissimilar reflections form one harmony or many, such are the favourite effects of Renoir – nor can we wonder that this infinite complexity of execution induces him to seek more hazardous success in things widely opposed to nature. A box at a theatre, its gaily-dressed inmates, the women with their flesh tints heightened and displayed by rouge and rice powder, a complication of effects of light – the more so when this scene is fantastically illuminated by an incongruous day-light. Such are the subjects he delights in.

All these various attempts and efforts (sometimes pushed yet farther by the intrepid M. de Césane) are united in the common bond of Impressionism. Incontestably honour is due to these who have brought to the service of art an extraordinary and quasi-original newness of vision, undeterred by a confused and hesitating age. If sometimes they have gone too far in the search of novel and audacious subjects, or have misapplied a freshly discovered principle, it is but another canvass turned to the wall; and as a set off to such an accident they have attained a praiseworthy result, to make us understand when looking on the most accustomed objects the delight that we should experience could we but see them for the first time.

If we try to recall some of the heads of our argument and to draw from them possible conclusions, we must first affirm that Impressionism is the principal and real movement of contemporary painting. The only one? No; since other great talents have been devoted to illustrate some particular phrase or period of bygone art; among these we must class such artists as Moreau, Puvis de Chavannes, etc.

At a time when the romantic tradition of the first half of the century only lingers among a few surviving masters of that time, the transition from the old imaginative artist and dreamer to the energetic modern worker is found in Impressionism.

The participation of a hitherto ignored people in the political life of France is a social fact that will honour the whole of the close of the nineteenth century. A parallel is found in artistic matters, the way being prepared by an evolution which the public with rare prescience dubbed, from its first appearance, Intransigeant, which in political language means radical and democratic.

The noble visionaries of other times, whose works are the semblance of worldly things seen by unworldly eyes, (not the actual representations of real objects) appear as kings and gods in the far dream-ages of mankind; recluses to whom were given the genius of a dominion over an ignorant multitude. But to-day the multitude demands to see with its own eyes; and if our latter-day art is less glorious, intense, and rich, it is not without the compensation of truth, simplicity and child-like charm.

At that critical hour for the human race when nature desires to work for herself, she requires certain lovers of hers – new and impersonal men placed directly in communion with the sentiment of their time – to loose the restraint of education, to let hand and eye do what they will, and thus through them, reveal herself.

For the mere pleasure of doing so? Certainly not, but to express herself, calm, naked, habitual, to those newcomers of to-morrow, of which each one will consent to be an unknown unit in the mighty numbers of an universal suffrage, and to place in their power a newer and more succinct means of observing her.

Such, to those who can see in this the representative art of a period which cannot isolate itself from the equally characteristic politics and industry, must seem the meaning of the manner of painting which we have discussed here, and which although marking a general phase of art has manifested itself particularly in France.

Now in conclusion I must hastily re-enter the domain of aesthetics, and I trust we shall thoroughly have considered our subject when I have shown the relation of the present crisis – the appearance of the Impressionists – to the actual principles of painting – a point of great importance.

In extremely civilized epochs the following necessity becomes a matter of course, the development of art and thought having nearly reached their far limits – art and thought are obliged to retrace their own footsteps, and to return to their ideal source, which never coincides with their real beginnings. English Praeraphaelitism, if I do not mistake, returned to the primitive simplicity of mediaeval ages. The scope and aim (not proclaimed by authority of dogmas, yet not the less clear), of Manet and his followers is that painting shall be steeped again in its cause, and its relation to nature. But what, except to decorate the ceilings of saloons and palaces with a crowd of idealized types in magnificent foreshortening, what can be the aim of a painter before everyday nature? To imitate her? Then his best effort can never equal the original with the inestimable advantages of life and space. – 'Ah no! this fair face, that green landscape, will grow old and wither, but I shall have them always, true as nature, fair as remembrance, and imperishably my own; or the better to satisfy my creative artistic instinct, that which I preserve through the power of Impressionism is not the material portion which already exists, superior to any mere representation of it, but the delight of having recreated nature touch by touch. I leave the massive and tangible solidity to its fitter exponent, sculpture. I content myself with reflecting on the clear and durable mirror of painting, that which perpetually lives yet dies every moment, which only exists by the will of Idea, yet constitutes in my domain the only authentic and certain merit of nature – the Aspect. It is through her that when rudely thrown at the close of an epoch of dreams in the front of reality, I have taken from it only that which properly belongs to my art, an original and exact perception which distinguishes for itself the things it perceives with the steadfast gaze of a vision restored to its simplest perfection.'

2 Le Jury de Peinture pour 1874 et M. Manet

This is the first of Mallarmé's texts directly concerned with painting and it is a clear, powerfully ironic defence of Manet. It was published on 12 April 1874 in 'La Renaissance Artistique et Littéraire'. It probably dates from the beginning of Mallarmé's friendship with Manet. The article hinges on a critique of the way the *Salon* jury acted as a mediator between the artist and the public. Mallarmé comments on several of Manet's painting and refutes many of the criticisms then aimed both at Manet and at *plein-air* painting.

Le Jury de Peinture pour 1874 et M. Manet

Tous ceux que l'approche du Salon émeut de quelque curiosité et les amateurs qui tournent les yeux vers des ateliers nouveaux ont, ces jours derniers, appris, très brusquement, que le jury de peinture écarte deux tableaux sur trois, envoyés par M. Manet.

La déception est grande pour plusieurs, même placés dans la foule, de ne pas étudier, cette année, la manifestation totale d'un talent exceptionnel; et les ennemis irréconciliables de visées neuves n'ont, eux, qu'a s'écrier «Pourquoi n'a-t-on pas refusé tout l'envoi?»

Je partage, quant à moi, le sentiment des premiers et je m'associe absolument à l'exclamation des autres.

Si l'on veut soustraire aux visiteurs du Salon le spectacle d'une peinture qui les inquiéta parfois (comme toute révélation dont le mot est encore obscur), autant qu'écarter d'eux le danger de se laisser peu à peu convaincre par des qualités éclatantes, il faut, certes, avoir le courage d'abuser pleinement et absolument, d'un pouvoir conféré dans un autre but. Ces habitudes anciennes et quelque temps oubliées, de régenter le goût de la foule, pourquoi ne les évoquer qu'à demi, et soit même aux deux tiers? (il y a peut-être, par leur fait, à sauver l'Art, comme tout autre chose.)

Toutefois, on pourrait, pour n'étonner personne que les membres du jury, arguer que le cas est plus ordinaire et que deux des toiles présentées par le peintre offraient de tels défauts, comparées à la troisième, que l'acceptation était impossible. Telle, malgré l'apparence d'absurdité impliquée par ces paroles, est, en effet, la suggestion proposée à la masse par le verdict prononcé tout à l'heure. Pas d'exclusion systématique, vous le voyez! il y a même jugement.

Quant à moi, par le seul fait que ces lignes paraissent quelque part où l'on s'occupe d'art, je craindrais d'humilier ces Messieurs; groupe de peintres habiles avant d'être des hommes maladroits, en jouant simplement la duperie: et j'aime, par quelque déférence, incriminer, plutôt que leur clairvoyance technique, la mauvaise foi apportée par eux dans l'usage d'un mandat échu en leurs mains. Quelque chose de fâcheux, cela fût-il faux, ressort de l'une de ces accusations: la seconde, je le sais, s'esquive par un sourire.

Pourquoi ne pas faire naître ce sourire?

M. Manet, pour une Académie (et j'ai nommé ce que, chez nous, malheureusement, devient tout conciliabule officiel) est, au point de vue de l'exécution non moins que de la conception de ses tableaux, un danger. La simplification apportée par un regard de voyant, tant il est positif! à certains procédés de la peinture dont le tort principal est de voiler l'origine de cet art fait d'onguents et de couleurs, peut tenter les sots séduits par une apparence de facilité. Quant au public, arrêté, lui, devant la reproduction immédiate de sa personnalité multiple, va-t-il ne plus jamais détourner les yeux de ce miroir pervers ni les reporter sur les magnificences allégoriques des plafonds ou les panneaux approfondis par un paysage, sur l'Art idéal et sublime. Si le moderne allait nuire à l'Éternel!

Telle est évidemment la pensée du plus grand nombre des peintres composant le jury, enfantine dans un cas, puérile dans l'autre, et qui n'est absolument déplacée (en égard à mille choses) que s'ils veulent l'immiscer en quoi que ce soit à leurs jugements.

Comment et sous quels prétextes, passer maintenant de cet te théorie à des actes.

Trois tableaux présentés par l'intrus redoutable: *le Bal de l'Opéra*, *les Hirondelles* et *le Chemin de fer* (figs 14–16). Sur les trois, un, *le Bal*, capital dans l'œuvre du peintre et y marquant comme un point culminant d'où l'on résume mainte tentative ancienne, était, certes, l'ouvrage qu'il y avait le moins lieu d'exposer à un succès unanime; quant au deuxième, *les Hirondelles*, très singulier pour un œil d'amateur et doué d'une séduction calme, on pouvait le faire passer pour moins significatif. Celui-ci rejeté de pair avec celui-là, telle a donc été l'idée: afin de paraître ne pas réserver toutes les rigueurs à l'œuvre accentuée, mais, frapper avec une égale sévérité, quelque chose même de vague! . . . Comme la sagesse la plus profonde ne prévoit pas tout et que ses desseins manquent toujours par quelque point, restait le troisième tableau, important lui-même sous un aspect trompeur et riche en suggestion pour qui aime à regarder. Je crois que cette toile échappée aux ruses et aux combinaisons des organisateurs du Salon, leur réserve encore une autre surprise, quand ce qu'il y aura à dire à son sujet aura été dit par ceux qu'intéressent certaines questions, notamment de métier pur.

Affaire du compte rendu qui sera fait ici-même du Salon: quant aux deux œuvres refusées, revenues demain aux galeries particulières où les attend leur place, il y a à les discuter, non pas avec le jury qui me dicterait au besoin mes appréciations, mais devant le public manquant de toute base pour asseoir sa conviction.

Rendre un coin du Bal de l'Opéra: quels étaient le périles à éviter dans l'accomplissement de certe audace? Le tapage discordant de costumes qui ne sont pas des toilettes et la gesticulation ahurie qui n'est celle d'aucun temps et d'aucun lieu, et n'offre pas à l'art plastique un répertoire d'attitudes authentiquement humaines. Les masques ne font donc, dans le tableau, que rompre, par quelques tons de frais bouquets, la monotonie possible du fond d'habits noirs; et ils disparaissent suffisamment pour qu'on ne voie en ce stationnement sérieux de promeneurs au foyer qu'un rendez-vous propre à montrer l'allure d'une foule moderne, laquelle ne saurait être peinte sans les quelques notes claires contribuant à l'égayer. Irréprochable est l'esthétique et, quant à la facture de ce morceau que les exigences de l'uniforme contemporain rendaient si parfaitement difficile, je ne crois pas qu'il y ait lieu de faire autre chose que de s'étonner de la gamme délicieuse trouvée dans les noirs: fracs et dominos, chapeaux et loups, velours, drap, satin et soie. A peine l'œil se figure-t-il la nécessité des notes vives ajoutées par les travestissements: il ne les distingue qu'attiré et retenu d'abord par le seul charme de la couleur grave et harmonieuse que fait un groupe *formé presque exclusivement d'hommes*. Rien donc de désordonné et de scandaleux quant à la peinture, et qui veuille comme sortir de la toile: mais, au contraire, la noble tentative d'y faire tenir, par de purs moyens demandés à cet art, toute vision du monde contemporain.

Quant aux Hirondelles, j'accorde à la plus superficielle des critiques une seule objection, afin de la réduire tout à l'heure. Deux dames assises sur l'herbe d'une de ces dunes du Nord de la France, s'étendant à l'horizon fermé derrière lequel on sent la mer, tant est vaste l'atmosphere qui entoure les deux personnages. Viennent de ce lointain des hirondelles donner son titre au tableau. L'impression de plein air se fait jour d'abord; et ces dames, tout à elles-mêmes dans leur songerie ou leur contemplation, ne sont d'ailleurs que des accessoires en la composition, comme il sied que les perçoive dans un si grand espace l'œil du peintre, arrêté à la seule harmonie de leurs étoffes grises et d'une après-midi de septembre.

Je signalais une réserve, faite à un point de vue d'école par qui ne tiendrait aucun compte de quelques remarques précédentes: elle consiste, si l'on veut, en ceci que, pour parler argot «le tableau n'est pas assez poussé» ou fini. Il y a longtemps que l'existence de cette plaisanterie me semble révoquée en doute par ceux qui la proférèrent d'abord. Qu'est-ce qu'une œuvre «pas assez poussé» alors qu'il y a entre tous ses éléments un accord par quoi elle se tient et possède un charme facile à rompre par une touche ajoutéé? Je pourrais, désireux de me montrer explicite, faire observer que, du reste, cette mesure, appliquée à la valeur d'un tableau, sans étude préalable de la dose d'impressions qu'il comporte, devrait, logiquement, atteindre l'excès dans le fini comme dans la lâché: tandis que, par une inconséquence singulière, on ne voit jamais l'humeur des juges sévir contre une toile, insignifiante et à la fois minutieuse jusqu'à l'effroi.

Le public, frustré dans son droit d'admiration ou de raillerie, sait maintenant tout: il ne reste en son nom qu'à formuler une question d'intérêt général, suggérée par l'aventure.

La question qu'il s'agissait de résoudre une fois de plus, et avec la même inutilité que toujours, tient tout entière dans ces mots: quel est, dans le double jugement rendu et par le jury et par le public sur la peinture de l'année, la tâche qui incombe au jury et celle qui relève de la foule?

Il résulte du seul fait de la mise en commun des talents notoires d'une époque, dont chacun possède nécessairement une originalité très différente, que l'accord susceptible entre eux porte non sur l'originalité, mais sur le talent même abstrait et exact, contenu dans l'œuvre à juger. Tous les artistes ont, indécise quelquefois dans la solitude du travail, mais arrêtée au contact les uns des autres, un sentiment très neutre de la valeur artistique discernable dans toute chose où elle se trouve: produit précieux et dont, seul, l'apport leur est demandé dans le cas présent. L'esprit dans lequel a été conçu un morceau d'art, rétrospectif ou moderne, et sa nature, succulente ou raréfiée, en un mot, tout ce qui touche aux instincts de la foule ou de la personne: c'est au public, qui paye en gloire et en billets, à décider se cela vaut son papier et ses paroles. Il est le maître à ce point, et peut exiger de voir *tout ce qu'il y a*. Chargé par le vote indistinct des peintres de choisir, entre les peintures présentées dans un cadre, ce qu'il existe véritablement, de tableaux, pour nous les mettre sous les yeux, le jury n'a d'autre chose à dire que: ceci est un tableau, ou encore: voilà qui n'est point un tableau. Défense d'en cacher un: dès que certaines tendances, latentes jusqu'alors dans le public ont trouvé, chez un peintre, leur expression artistique, ou leur beauté, il faut que celui-là fasse connaissance de celui-ci; et ne pas présenter l'un à l'autre est faire d'une maladresse un mensonge et une injustice.

La maladresse demeure heureusement dans le cas présent; et telle! qu'elle suffit à effacer les mots graves que vient de proférer la logique. Oui, il s'offrait aux retardataires de toutes les écoles, qui se sont partagé le succès pendant ces dernières années, une occasion parfaite de montrer au seul homme qui ait tenté de s'ouvrir à lui et à la peinture une voie nouvelle, que certes, un attachement à des points de vue anciens mais n'ayant peut-être pas encore livré tout leur secret, les tenait au cœur fortement, et non pas une cécité totale quant au présent. On a cru avoir à fermer les yeux davantage: gratuitement. Le jour où le public, lassé, se lassera tout à fait, que faire, sans l'appât destiné, dans de sages prévisions, à contenter le juste goût du neuf? La foule, à qui l'on ne cèle rien, vu que tout émane d'elle, se reconnaîtra, une autre fois, dans l'œuvre accumulée et survivante: et son détachement des choses passées n'en sera cette fois, que plus absola. Gagner quelques années sur M. Manet: triste politique!

Ce maître nouveau, qu'on a vu, dans une pensée supérieure et avec une sagacité mal comprise, présenter annuellement le développement de sa manière, toujours de plus en plus accusé et de plus en plus antipathique, par conséquent, avait le droit d'attendre que le sousentendu, impliqué par sa démarche, fût compris, à la longue, de juges délicats et soucieux de rien autre chose que du talent.

Le jury a préféré se donner ce ridicule de faire croire, pendant quelques jours encore, qu'il avait charge d'âmes.

3   Preface to the catalogue of the posthumous exhibition of Berthe Morisot's paintings, held at the Durand-Ruel Gallery, Paris from 5–23 March, 1896

The text is reproduced here with the same spatial arrangement of paragraphs as the original pamphlet. One of Manet's portraits of Morisot (fig. 40) appeared as frontispiece. Mallarmé evokes Morisot's life and work, and the exhibition itself, in poetic prose in which a fair amount of factual information is embedded. It is a celebration of Morisot as a painter which includes passages where Mallarmé transposes the structures and effects of her painting into words. In this respect it goes beyond either of Mallarmé's other principal texts on painting.

Préface

Tant de clairs tableaux irisés, ici, exacts, primesautiers, eux peuvent attendre avec le sourire futur, consentiront que comme titre au livret qui les classe, un Nom, avant de se résoudre en leur qualité, pour lui-même prononcé ou le charme extraordinaire avec lequel il fut porté, évoque une figure de race, dans la vie et de personnelle élégance extrêmes. Paris la connut peu, si sienne, par lignée et invention dans la grâce, sauf à des rencontres comme celle-ci, fastes, les expositions ordinairement de Monet et Renoir, quelque part où serait un Degas, devant Puvis de Chavannes ou Whistler, plusieurs les hôtes du haut salon, le soir; en la matinée, atelier très discret, dont les lambris Empire encastrèrent des toiles d'Édouard Manet. Quand, à son tour, la dame y peignait-elle, avec furie et nonchalance, des ans, gardant la monotonie et, dégageant à profusion une fraîcheur d'idée, il faut dire – toujours – hormis ces réceptions en l'intimité où, le matériel de travail relégué, l'art même était loin quoique immédiat dans une causerie égale au décor, ennobli du groupe: car un Salon, surtout, impose, avec quelques habitués, par l'absence d'autres, la pièce, alors, explique son élévation et confère, de plafonds altiers, la supériorité à la gardeinne, là, de l'espace si, comme c'était, énigmatique de paraître cordiale et railleuse ou accueillant selon le regard scrutateur levé de l'attente, distinguée, sur quelque meuble bas, la ferveur. Prudence aux quelques-uns d'apporter une bonhomie, sans éclat, un peu en comparses sachant parmi ce séjour, raréfié dans l'amitié et le beau, quelque chose, d'étrange planer, qu'ils sont venus pour indiquer de leur petit nombre, la luxueuse, sans même y penser, exclusion de tout le dehors.

Cette particularité d'une grande artiste qui, non plus, comme maîtresse de maison, ne posséda rien de banal, causait, aux présentations, presque la gêne. Pourquoi je cède, pour attarder une réminiscence parfaite, bonne, défunte, comme sitôt nous la résumions précieusement au sortir, dans les avenues du Bois ou des Champs-Élysées, tout à coup à me mémorer ma satisfaction, tel minuit, de lire en un compagnon de pas, la même timidité que, chez moi, longtemps, envers l'amicale méduse, avant le parti gai de tout brusquer par un dévouement. «Auprès de Madame Manet» concluait le paradoxal confident, un affiné causeur entre les grands jeunes poëtes et d'aisé maintien, «je me fais l'effet d'un rustre et une brute» Pareil mot, que n'ouït pas l'intéressée, ne se redira plus. Comme toute remarque très subtile appartient aux feuillets de la fréquentation, les entr'ouvrir à moitié, livre ce qui se doit, d'un visage, au temps: relativement à l'exception, magnifique, dans la sincérité du retirement qui élut une femme du monde à part soi; puis se précise un fait de la société, il semble, maintenant.

Les quelques dissidentes du sexe qui présentent l'esthétique autrement que par leut individu, au reste, encourent un défaut, je ne désigne pas de traiter avec sommaire envahissement le culte que, peut-être, confisquons-nous au nom d'études et de la rêverie, passons une concurrence des prêtresses avisées; mais quand l'art s'en mêle, au contraire, de dédaigner notre pudeur qui allie visée et dons chez chacun et, tout droit, de bondir au sublime, éloigné, certes, gravement, au rude, au fort: elles nous donnent une leçon de virilité et, aussi, déchargeraient les institutions officielles ou d'État, en soignant la notion de vastes maquettes éternelles, dont le goût, de se garer, à moins d'illumination spéciale. – Une juvénilité constante absout l'emphase. – Que la pratique plairait, efficace, si visant, pour les transporter vers plus de rareté, encore et d'essence, les délicatesses, que nous nous contraignons d'avoir presque féminines. A ce jeu s'adonna, selon le tact d'une arrière-petite-nièce, en descendance, de Fragonard, Mme Berthe Morisot, naguères apparentée à l'homme, de ce temps, qui rafraîchit la tradition française – par mariage avec un frère, M. Eugène Manet, esprit très perspicase et correct. Toujours, délicieusement, aux manifestations pourchassées de l'Impressionnisme – la source, en peinture, vive – un panneau, revoyons-le, en 1874, 1876, 1877, 1883, limpide, frissonnant empaumait à des carnations, à des vergers, à des ciels, à toute la légèreté du métier avec une pointe du XVIIIe siècle exaltée de présent, la critique, attendrie pour quelque chose de moins péremptoire que l'entourage et de'élyséennement savoureux: erreur, une acuité interdisant ce bouquet, déconcertait la bienveillance. Attendu, il importe, que la fascination dont on aimerait profiter, superficiellement et à travers de la présomption, ne s'opère qu'à des conditions intègres et même pour le passant hostiles; comme regret. Toute maîtrise jette le froid: ou la poudre fragile du coloris se défend par une vitre, divination pour certains.

Telle, de bravoure, une existence allait continuer, insoucieuse, après victoire et dans l'hommage; quand la prévision faillit, durant l'hiver, de 1895, aux frimas tardifs, voici les douze mois revenus: la ville apprit que cette absente, en des magies, se retirait plus avant soit suprêmement, au gré d'un malaise de la saison. Pas, dans une sobriété de prendre congé sans insistance ou la cinquantaine avivant une expression, bientôt, souvenir: on savait la personne de prompt caprice, pour conjurer l'ennui, singulière, apte dans les résolutions; mais elle n'eût pas accueilli celle-là de mourir, plutôt que conserver le cercle fidèle, à cause, passionnément, d'une ardente flamme maternelle, où se mit, en entier, la créatrice – elle subit, certes, l'apitoiement ou la torture, malgré la force d'âme, envisageant l'heure inquiète d'abandonner, hors un motif pour l'une et l'autre de séparation, près le chevalet, une très jeune fille, de deux sangs illustre, à ses propres espoirs joignant la belle fatalité de sa mère et des Manet. Consignons l'étonnement des journaux à relater d'eux-mêmes, comme un détail notoire pour les lecteurs, le vide, dans l'art, inscrit par une disparue auparavant réservée: en raison, soudain, de l'affirmation, dont quiconque donne avis, à l'instant salua cette renommée tacite.

Si j'ai inopportunément, prélude aux troimphe et délice, hélas! anniversaires, obscurci par le deuil, des traits invités à reformer la plus noble physionomie, je témoigne d'un tort, accuse la défaillance convenable aux tristesses: l'impartiale visiteuse, aujourd'hui, de ses travaux, ne le veut ni, elle-même, entre tous ces portraits, intercepter du haut d'une chevelure blanchie par l'abstraite épuration en le beau plus qu'âgée, avec quelque longueur de voile, un jugement, foyer serein de vision ou n'ayant pas besoin, dans la circonstance, du recul de la mort: sans ajouter que ce serait, pour l'artiste, en effet, verser dans tel milieu en joie, en fête et en fleur, la seule ombre qui, par elle, y fût jamais peinte et que son pinceau récusait.

Ici, que s'évanouissent, dispersant une caresse radieuse, idyllique, fine, poudroyante, diaprée, comme en ma mémoire, les tableaux, reste leur armature, maint superbe dessin, pas de moindre instruction, pour attester une science dans la volontaire griffe, couleurs à part, sur un sujet – ensemble trois cents ouvrages environ, et études qu'au public d'apprécier avec le sens, vierge, puisé à ce lustre nacré et argenté: faut-il, la hantise de suggestions, aspirant à se traduire en l'occasion, la taire, dans la minute, suspens de perpétuité chatoyante? Silence, excepté que paraît un spectacle d'enchantement moderne. Loin ou dès la croisée qui prépare à l'extérieur et maintient, dans une attente verte d'Hespérides aux simples oranges et parmi la brique rose d'Eldorados, tout à coup l'irruption à quelque carafe, éblouissamment du jour, tandis que multicolore il se propage en perses et en tapis réjouis, le génie, distillateur de la Crise, où cesse l'étincelle des chimères au mobilier, est, d'abord, d'un peintre. Poétiser, par art plastique, moyen de prestiges directs, semble, sans intervention, le fait de l'ambiance éveillant aux surfaces leur lumineux secret: ou la riche analyse, chastement pour la restaurer, de la vie, selon une alchimie, – mobilité et illusion. Nul éclairage, intrus, de rêves; mais supprimés, par contre, les aspects commun ou professionnel. Soit, que l'humanité exulte, en tant que les chairs de préférence chez l'enfant, fruit, jusqu'au bouton de la nubilité, là tendrement finit cette célébration de nu, notre contemporaine aborde sa semblable comme il ne faut l'omettre, la créature de gala, agencée en vue d'usages étrangers, galbeuse ou fignolée relevant du calligraphe à moins que le genre n'induise, littérairement, le romancier; à miracle, elle la restitue, par quelle clairvoyance, le satin se vivifiant à un contact de peau, l'orient des perles, à l'atmosphère: ou, dévêt, en négligé idéal, la mondanité fermée au style, pour que jaillisse l'intention de la toilette dans un rapport avec les jardins et la plage, une serre, la galerie. Le tour classique renoué et ces fluidité, nitidité.

Féerie, oui, quotidienne – sans distance, par l'inspiration, plus que le plein air enflant un glissement, le matin ou après-midi, de cygnes à nous; ni au-delà que ne s'acclimate, des ailes détournée et de tous paradis, l'enthousiaste innéité de la jeunesse dans une profondeur de journée.

Rappeler, indépendamment des sortilèges, la magicienne, tout à l'heure obéit à un souhait, de concordance, qu'elle-même choya, d'être aperçue par autrui comme elle se pressentit: on peut dire que jamais elle ne manqua d'admiration ni de solitude. Plus, pourquoi – il faut regarder les murs – au sujet de celle dont l'éloge courant veut que son talent dénote la femme – encore, aussi, qu'un maître: son œuvre, achevé, selon l'estimation des quelques grands originaux qui la comptèrent comme camarade dans la lutte, vaut, à côté d'aucun, produit par un d'eux et se lie, exquisement, à l'histoire de la peinture, pendant une époque du siècle.

4   Courbet, *Le Sommeil*, 1866

5   Regnault, *Salomé*, 1871

6   Moreau, *Fleur Mystique*, c.1875

7   Puvis de Chavannes, *Beheading of John the Baptist*, 1869

> Mais langoureusement longe
> Comme de blanc linge ôté
> Tel fugace oiseau si plonge
> Exultatrice à côté
>
> Dans l'onde toi devenue
> Ta jubilation nue.   Mallarmé, 'Petit Air'

'The Impressionists and Edouard Manet' is constructed around Manet's painting *Le Linge*, (fig. 3) which Mallarmé described as 'a complete and final repertory of all current ideas and the means of their execution', the culmination of a series of innovations which 'marks a date in a lifetime, perhaps, but certainly one in the history of art' (72). Yet the painting is an informal treatment of a domestic scene, a moment so specific that you can see the water running out of the cloth as the woman wrings it. Like the gleams of stormy light at the beginning of 'Crise de Vers', the monumental is a quality which subsists in divergent details, intensely focused. That sense of deflection, of the introduction of a different sense of time which alters the relation of the individual to the historical, is the principal thread in both essays. Impressionism and *vers libre* are seen to mark a definitive break with the past, a suspension constituting the major development of the century in change, the present moment becoming a relation between an unknown future and what it makes of the past.

In 'The Impressionists and Edouard Manet' Mallarmé recognises that post-Romantic art had been succeeded by divergent developments. These are signalled by his starting point with Courbet (fig. 4) and 'the decorative', exemplified by Regnault (fig. 5). In his conclusion, however, with Moreau (fig. 6) and Puvis de Chavannes (figs. 7 and 50) who are understood to be compatible on some level with Manet and Impressionism, Mallarmé seeks to understand the reality which produces the divergence. Both here and in 'Crise de Vers' his analysis is aimed at defining the nature of the post-Romantic crisis, its immediate antecedents and its probable consequences in formal and epistemological terms. In this he locates one rupture and resultant shift, of which the various 'schools' and styles are separate manifestations. 'Décadente, Mystique, les Écoles se déclarent ou étiquetées en hâte par notre presse d'information.' (365). He begins to define the search for a polymorphic form through which a complete experiential idea might be externalised, the sensible, pure notion or idea or 'Aspect' (capitalised in the text of 'The Impressionists and Edouard Manet'). It is defined in various ways in all the essays and in most in 'The Impressionists and Edouard Manet', and 'Crise de Vers', which extends its predecessor on all levels to elaborate the problematic and its dominant metaphor of light. 'Crise de Vers' is more complex and it builds up a nexus of minimally indicated concepts, basically the material, the real, the source (historical and immediate), the perceptible, the intelligible, the expressible, the individual and the collective. And although it is all haunted by idealist thinking it is in equipoise between idealism, touching on the Platonic and German varieties, and another more diffuse non-essentialist kind of trans-realism. Light and air fascinate Mallarmé as the least material of material media and as the most appropriate figures for what in 'The Impressionists and Edouard Manet' is summarised as 'the Aspect' (sic) and the 'ideal source'. These are at once both ends of the historical–present, real–ideal continuum. Light emphasises the immediate, air the non-immediate, and the difficulty of separating them in time signals the quality of their seemingly inaccessible or intangible reality.

Manet is described as the exponent of a Naturalism derived not from 'that reality which impresses itself in its abstract form on all' but 'from a direct sentiment of nature' (67). His work has a 'peculiar quality outside mere realism' (68), its truths reveal Nature as 'new and strange' (72) depriving reality of its solidity and materialising the vital processes of light and air (74–5). In this, art is neither ideal nor imitation (85) but 'an original and exact perception which distinguishes for itself the thing it perceives with the steadfast gaze of a vision restored to its simplest perfection' (86).

A large part of Mallarmé's argument is directed towards analysing Manet's problem-solving. 'Each work should be a new creation of the mind . . . Such a result cannot be attained all at once. To reach it the master must pass through many phases ere this self-isolation can be acquired and this new evolution of art be learnt' (69). Manet's development is described as a process, or as successive attempts to surmount obstacles, chiefly those of code, the 'personal' and the 'material' both in terms of media (paint, handling etc.) and in philosophical terms. What I take Mallarmé to be saying is that the material means of art are to be actively involved in a dynamic sense of experience as a point between traversing realities. Given equal semantic weight as subject-matter, every mark on the canvas is a carrier of meaning analogous with the phoneme.[6] Mallarmé stresses that the scattered pre-existence of technical processes and effects, 'borrowings' of structures or figures, does not at all detract from the novelty of Manet's Impressionism, which assembles them in such a way as to expose what would be 'the dialectic of the sign', and its dialectic in turn with history. It is an approach to the formal and to the imaginary which moves from external reality, physical and perceptible properties to 'Mystery' without a break, with 'mere realism', abstract reality, ironically cast aside together with 'the old imaginative artist and dreamer' (84–6). But Manet's achievement for Mallarmé was to synthesise the immediate – 'that absolute and important sentiment which Nature herself impresses on all those who have voluntarily abandoned conventionalism' (67) – with a full knowledge of the past. The two currents, out of Courbet on the one hand, and the mythological or allusive painters (Moreau, Puvis, Pre-Raphaelites) on the other, may give access to an originality beyond the individual, the kind of mythic transcendence in terms of which Mallarmé described his own language, and which I would describe as freeing Subjectivity:

8   Manet, *Un Déjeuner sur l'Herbe*, 1863

But the chief charm and true characteristic of one of the most singular men of the age is that Manet (who is a visitor to the principal galleries both French and foreign and an erudite student of painting) seems to ignore all that had been done in art by others and to draw from his own inner consciousness all his effects of simplification, the whole revealed by effects of light incontestably novel. This is the supreme originality of a painter by whom originality is doubly forsworn, who seeks to lose his personality in Nature herself, or in the gaze of a multitude until then ignorant of her charms.   (78)

'Nature' is thus made visible through art on the one hand and innate but transformable structures of the mind on the other. 'The gaze of the multitude' here, as in Mallarmé's earlier essay on Manet, 'Le Jury de Peinture pour 1874 et M. Manet' (figs. 14, 15, 16) is not only those who look at the painting, but also the artist's contemporaries overall, and, through the 'dialectic of the sign' the distillation of what it has been possible to see and say previously, the knowledge of earlier cultural production transmitted in Manet's experimentation, 'the assemblage for the first time of all these relative processes for an end, visible and suitable to the artistic expression of the needs of our time' (77–8).

Mallarmé's account thus attempts to outline a case for Manet's Impressionism as marking a definitive shift which involves the transformation of the means of representation and of consciousness of Nature as a kind of 'realism' whose means derive from a synthesis of perceptual description and extreme formal sophistication. The formal argument is central – that is, Mallarmé assesses the culmination of Manet's series of technical experiments as achieving the objectification of what

9　Manet, *Le Bon Bock*, 1873

12　Manet, *Argenteuil*, 1874

10　Manet, *L'Exécution de l'Empereur Maximilien*, 1867

13　Manet, *Le Balcon*, 1868–9

11　Manet, *En Bateau*, 1874

14   Manet, *Le Bal, de l'Opéra*, 1873

15   Manet, *Les Hirondelles*, 1873

16   Manet, *Le Chemin de Fer*, 1873

Mallarmé calls 'inner' consciousness and this is where he is truly an innovator. The recording of immediate perception and its 'perpetual metamorphosis' is crucially different from what had gone before, even where apparent parallels would seem to exist. The Impressionist method of fragmentation and remaking transforms the perceiving mind by introducing a self-conscious distance between seer and seen.

The woman and child in *Le Linge*, for example, are painted with flat broad strokes and summary lines to indicate details. The child is like a cylinder with its eye smudgily indicated in dark blue. The leaves and bushes around are filled with movement, painted with apparently free touches while depicting the tangled plant forms naturalistically. Yet the paint is totally undisguised, each mark announcing itself as such. The foreground particularly is painted with a calligraphic brevity reminiscent of Whistler, who is also mentioned, and who was to become a close friend.

The major structural device in *Le Linge* is also used by Whistler and is perhaps one of the components of what Mallarmé calls 'the Japanese perspective' (to which I shall return). The spaces are closed off and divided, in this case with the sheets hung on the lines to dry. In the Japanese print it is more generally screen or wall-divisions, or some other theatrical or architectural feature: a balcony, multiple levels, or a partially obscured distant horizon. Manet and Whistler use many of these, with the addition of mirrors, as in *Un Bar aux Folies Bergères* (fig. 34), or in Whistler's *White Girl* series (figs. 35–37). Mallarmé mentions in this context the high horizon line in Manet's sea-pieces, perhaps meaning the *Kearsage and Alabama* (not illustrated) or *Les Hirondelles* (fig. 15), discussed in 'Le Jury de Peinture pour 1874 et M. Manet'. The painting he mentioned as marking one of Manet's developmental stages, *En Bateau*, (fig. 11) is, however, a striking example. Common to all these very different works is the spatial ambiguity introduced by the flattening effect of closure and the depth or depths of the contained spaces. In *Le Linge* (fig. 3), there are three areas closing off the scene, the two sheets on their lines (which could not in fact exist, it appears, in relation to one another) and the dark green foliage in the background, with a path from the bottom left corner leading towards the convergence-point of the two lines, and the indistinct area behind. The arrangement is thus apparently casual – the figures depicted in a suspended moment – and yet constructed with conspicuous artifice. The impact of this surprising perspectival manipulation is intensified in Manet by the scale – *Le Linge* and *En Bateau*, like many of his paintings, are life-size or larger, again, in contrast to the diminishing sizes of the landscapes painted by other Impressionists in pursuit of the fleeting effect of light.

The impact of Japanese art and artefacts on painters in France from the 1850s on is well known to art historians.[7] The Japanese print appeared 'natural', a direct visual record affording a method of quick notation of abbreviated forms, yet it also had a strangeness, a fantastic and theatrical realism arising from its spatial novelty and simplified colours and shapes.

In 'The Impressionists and Edouard Manet' Mallarmé touches on all the main

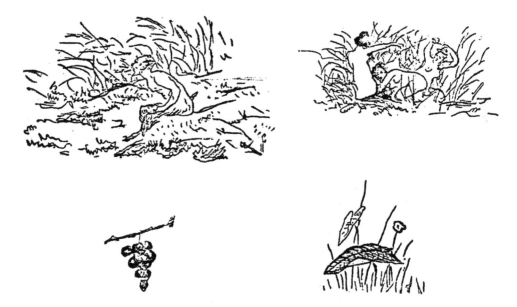

17–20 Manet, illustrations for 'L'Après-Midi d'un Faune', 1876

21 Hokusai, *Lily*, a sketch from *Mangwa*

22–27 Manet, illustrations for 'Le Corbeau', 1875

features associated with the Japanese – the abolition of formal composition, perspectival devices including informal 'snapshot' arrangements of subjects, simplification of forms, the dynamic construction of space using simple lines and size diminution instead of linear perspective combined with the tensions consequent on raising the horizon line to flatten the depth so created. His account places the Japanese as the second of the two major components of 'open air' painting as exemplified by *Le Linge*: 'atmosphere' (colour, the depiction of the perpetual oscillation between light, air and objects through touches of paint and the regulation of tone) and 'natural perspective', which includes containing space, the immediacy of 'one glance of a scene framed in by the hands', but also 'an absolutely new science' and 'the recovery of a long obliterated truth' (77). Clearly much of Mallarmé's admiration goes to Manet's achievement in depicting such effects as 'perceptual immediacy', but his point is that what Mallarmé calls 'that promptitude which just suffices for the connection of the truth' means that what is seen was not previously visible. Like the photograph its immediacy goes beyond that of encapsulating a scene, an awareness of optical selectivity – if appearances are in 'perpetual metamorphosis' (as in Mallarmé's description of *Le Linge*) and yet are perceived as stable, then seeing is an active, if partially unconscious, process, interrelated with cognition. The difference in code in the Japanese print emphasised the artificiality of Western conventions of representation, not by being more 'natural' but by presenting an alternative system. In this its impact was part of a larger re-evaluation, which was visible not only in what Mallarmé called Manet's 'divergent course' towards Spanish and Flemish painting (69) but in Moreau's and Puvis de Chavanne's devotion to the art of the past, and in the Pre-Raphaelites, who 'returned to the primitive simplicity of mediaeval ages' (85):

> In extremely civilised epochs the following necessity becomes a matter of course, the development of art and thought having nearly reached their far limits – art and thought are obliged to retrace their own footsteps, and to return to their ideal source which never coincides with their real beginnings. (85)

All these attempts may be seen as code-breaking 'deconstruction'. But the artists' collective impulse is to 'an original and exact perception which distinguishes for itself the things it perceives with the steadfast gaze of a vision restored to its simplest perfection' and 'the delight of having recreated nature touch by touch' (86).

The second principal means Mallarmé describes as provided by the Japanese perspective, or at least exemplified by it, is calligraphy. This relates written and pictorial expression, and is therefore, in the context of Western practice, transmutative. It is also summary, omits the 'personal obtrusion' Mallarmé deprecates, in allowing the free action of hand and eye. Both the sets of illustrations Manet executed for Mallarmé tend toward this mode (figs. 17–27) particularly those for his translation of 'The Raven' (figs. 22–27). The brushmark neither depicts an object nor expressive feeling – it is neither figurative, nor abstract, nor expressive. In

28   Manet, *Annabel Lee*

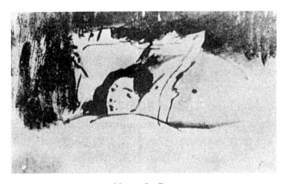

29   Manet, *La Dormeuse*

30   Manet, *La Cité en la Mer*

Japanese, certain ideophonic words are called 'sound gestures'.[8] Using intonation contour, the basic word-shape, allows the language user, most commonly the child, entry into the system of meanings because it permits discrimination between sound-sequences which have the power to express feeling and also to evoke a response in someone else. Emotion and desire can be discerned and then specified. Affect is therefore very prominent in initiating the meaning. Indeed, the evocative power of sound promotes affect as a structural and mnestic principle and is more 'expressive' in this sense than in the Romantic and subjective sense. Three of the most striking features of 'The Raven' work in this way: its insistent rhythm, its alliteration and its repetitious rhymes, and its refrain 'Nevermore'. Mallarmé's prose translation preserves this quality and exploits the evocative power of sound to the full:

Et le Corbeau, sans voleter, siège encore – siège encore sur le buste pallide de Pallas, juste au-dessus de la porte de ma chambre, et ses yeux ont toute la semblance des yeux d'un démon qui rêve, et la lumière de la lampe ruisselant sur lui, projette son ombre à terre: et mon âme, de cette ombre qui gît flottante à terre, ne s'élèvera – jamais plus!   (193)

Both Poe and Mallarmé experimented with the potential of sound to make new meaning by promoting this level of sound-shape through which meaning is first grasped.

Manet's brushwork in the illustrations for 'The Raven' and to some extent in *Le Linge* may be seen as a gestural sign which carries meaning in the sense just proposed. Manet's illustrations for both 'The Raven' and 'L'Après-Midi d'un Faune' appear to derive some of their calligraphic abbreviation from Hokusai, and like music, the calligraphic is a unitary introversive sign. Calligraphy, of course, is also hand-writing with varying degrees of representation in all non-alphabetic systems of notation. Writing as gestural sign is explored repeatedly in Mallarmé's texts where it is like an externalised memory trace as well as a medium. The brushmark or 'nervous handwriting'[9] in Impressionism, and in *Le Linge* specifically, is similarly part of a heterogeneous sign. In this painting and in 'The Raven' illustrations Manet appears to use the full range of transformations between the representational and introversive sign. Since 'The Raven' also combines narrative with the sound equivalent of calligraphy, Manet's illustrations are an excellent structural transposition[10] of the poem. The first of them depicts the narrator in his room according to the details of the poem and to conventional, though boldly sketch-like and free, representation. The brushmarks become increasingly prominent throughout the four, until in the last, the referential component is reduced to a minimum. Again, what the mark signifies is not affects – though they play a part in its determination – but the content of the somatic experience.

In 'The Impressionists and Edouard Manet', Mallarmé described the movement towards introversive signification – an aspect of what he calls the 'ideal source' – as one of Manet's main achievements in *Le Linge*. Both here and elsewhere Mallarmé's arguments tend towards interpreting it as a message without a code, although not in a simple or direct sense. Immediately before embarking on his analysis of *Le Linge* and open-air painting, for example, Mallarmé's argument shifts to the ex-centric. It is a movement which produces a peculiar tension characteristic of 'The Impressionists and Edouard Manet' overall, and at this point in his analysis of the Japanese perspective and 'open-air' painting in *Le Linge* it is very marked. It arises to some degree from the emergence in the essay of ideas that are still more far-reaching than its already considerable explicit argument. The 'digressions' and passages of relative opacity are therefore equally important both to the specific argument and to understanding where it fits into Mallarmé's own theory. It is not merely a question of illustrative metaphoric passages, restating and clarifying difficult points in the argument, as for example in 'L'Art pour tous' or in almost any of his discursive pieces setting forth an analysis or point of view. Nor is it poetic prose, as in 'Symphonie Littéraire' in which no critical distance is maintained by the writer from the material on which he is commenting. Instead the experience is reconstructed, not described. Perhaps it may be described as standing in the same relation to what we loosely (that is, not in the strict philosophical sense) call 'logical argument' as metonym[11] does to metaphor. In this it moves towards abstraction in some respects, most particularly in its transmutative character which is also common to Manet's painting and Mallarmé's poetry. Referring to *Le Repos*, (fig. 73) Mallarmé tries to make what he called 'an obscure and delicate point' about the depiction of women, who are 'by our civilisation consecrated to night'. Yet the point leads to another version of the 'ideal source' by means of which art and thought diverge, project themselves forward – the image of the woman, the exotic or the past as Other. Therefore the passage may be read on one level as referring to the interaction of the visible and the invisible in the sense of what cannot be directly known, or seen, or thought. The woman in the artificial, civilised setting is representative of this juncture, 'consecrated to night' while requiring to be 'admitted fresh and simple to the number of every day haunters of the imagination'. Open air and daylight lead Mallarmé immediately to their opposites, an interior (*Le Repos*) and night. To rearrange Mallarmé's words, 'the natural light of day penetrating into and influencing all things, although itself invisible' is the agent of a 'mental operation' through which the observer is enabled to 'fix on a mental canvas' a more accurate memory of what is seen. A comparison may be made with the clown in 'Le Pitre Châtié' who desires to escape his 'rance nuit de la peau' through his disguise and to turn sooty lamplight into daylight. The poem, using metaphors of light and the theatre, is about writing as transformative process – the histrionic gesture 'comme plume'. 'Open-air' painting depicts 'flesh-pollen', 'the special beauty which springs from the very source of life', and so by indirect means presents the unseen.

The attempt to articulate this 'mental operation' which underlies, or necessitates, technical innovation also leads to some hypothetical 'ideal source' in 'Crise de Vers':

Le souhait d'un terme de splendeur brillant, ou qu'il s'éteigne, inverse; quant à des alternatives lumineuses simples . . .

. . .

Arcane étrange; et d'intentions pas moindres, a jailli la métrique aux temps incubatoires.   (364).

Au traitement, si intéressant, par la versification subi, de repos et interrègne, gît, moins que dans nos
circonstances mentales vièrges, la crise.   (365)

Vers Libre, in this account, signifies 'la dissolution maintenant du nombre
officiel', and Mallarmé again attends to how this might allow the creation of a novel,
'polymorphic' line of verse, since a transition had to be effected, a new construction.

The artists who looked back beyond the Renaissance, to the medieval, or to
non-European cultures may be understood as pushing back the limits of the
knowable – not in order to retreat, but in order to discover a way forward. The
historical questions this raises are large. Mallarmé, Manet and the other artists
discussed in 'The Impressionists and Edouard Manet', in their deliberate refusal of
coherence or of certain codes hitherto accepted as clear and simple, participate in
socio-political upheaval. There is more than one form of 'art engagé', and more to
social development than political ideology, although this is not to deny their
importance. To separate and hierarchise certain forms of art can become a kind of
censorship. Formal experimentation, extreme subjectivity may equally be revo-
lutionary. 'History' in Mallarmé's account of Manet is not an ideological reflection;
perhaps the fact that they are often judged as flawed, having in some sense failed, is.
'History' in Manet is consciousness in struggle. The problematic nature of their
work is in itself a signifier. It will not become clear and simple if the right 'key' is
found (a whole generation of interesting critics were misled by this implicit or
explicit belief with Mallarmé). Mallarmé's and Manet's deliberate resistance to
certain forms (their structural breaks, for example) and to naturalisation often evokes
resistance in the potential receiver of their message. The drive of their text is
transgressive.

This means that the works stand in an oblique relation to their socio-historic
context rather than being 'transcendent' or 'absolute'. The same is true of what is
claimed as having an 'aesthetic effect'. There would seem to be some basis for the
aesthetic in innate structures, but it would also seem that what is innate has the
capacity to evolve and so does the range of possible response. This is further support
for the argument that formal discoveries and innovations – as according to
Formalism – are of immediate bearing on 'realism' and contemporary thought, and
are not separable into some branch of the immutable. The aesthetic is not the
exclusive property of 'high art', but is potentially as powerful and operative in the
folk tale as in the most refined poem – indeed without contact with its main-springs,
art is effete or degenerate, mere convention. As the twentieth century discovered,
aesthetic quality can be common to so-called primitive, ephemeral or unworked
'found' pieces and 'high' art alike, and is not in this sense exclusive. But the
'civilised' response to the 'primitive' work is not the same as the 'primitive', nor does
it enshrine the same values or make manifest the same power. When the 'civilised' or
dominant separates areas of different experience it deprives them of context and
renders them abnormal. The categorisation effectively represses or controls the
experiential.

The tension between conceptualisation and experience in Mallarmé is, however, dynamic. I mentioned above what he calls 'mythic transcendence' of language whereby speaker and spoken become other. The self-conscious distance is similarly past–presence, archetypal and yet compatible with learning in its essential. With the externalisation of a hitherto unconscious perceptual fact comes conceptual development. As with the written trace, described in *Tristes Tropiques* by Lévi-Strauss as constituting an irrevocable development for those people to whom it was previously unknown, the Impressionist perceptual trace records and launches into the world an internal fact. This necessitates cultural reassessment, since a new category cannot be simply added without altering the rest. In Derrida's terminology, 'différence' is a movement in time and space. Initially, it will act as a break or a contradiction, but it will not lack meaning. It will presignify. This is consistent with the explicitly broader implication of Derrida's self-miming history in *La Double Séance*, the rapport between reproducer and reproduced being to the present past. It is necessary to be able to think of the imitation as preceding the model, or at least of the simultaneity of the realisation of the one and the dissipation of the other. Mallarmé's 'perpetual metamorphosis', his description of the Impressionist portrayal of light, is imaged in points of light in his own verse (the chandelier, constellation or page), allomorphs of the active white on the page in reading.

In Manet's paintings, in which there is no attempt to hide his references, no smoothness or pictorial 'construction', may be seen the deliberate assembly of elements from apparently unrelated sources, constituting not a private language or breakdown in the sense of ceasing to function, but rather a denial of connoted meaning. Thus the new relation in which traditional or conventional signifiers are placed, generating meaning or a new sign, redefines its relation with the past and present. Mallarmé's description of Manet's development is of this order, a process and necessary departure moving towards the reinvention of painted signs which should be capable of assimilating and transforming their constituents into a point of intersection, a new sign.

There is a parallel with Mallarmé's analysis in the fundamental conceptual category which Barthes proposes as having been initiated by photography – the temporal paradox of a message without a code which is therefore capable of preserving an illusion of past-presence.[12] In Mallarmé's theory, the concept would be generalised into a principle of which photography would be a symptom. It would not matter whether it existed because it is the potential that matters. The obliteration of the poet in words and the painter in the action of eye and hand affords an autonomy of the written and painted text analogous to that of the photographic text.

The language of the paintings Mallarmé describes as marking stages in Manet's development (*Olympia* (fig. 71), *Un Déjeuner sur l'herbe* (fig. 8) etc; 71–2) and others like them in allusive construction, is transitional, a means towards making the Impressionist optical language possible, since they present only the notion, rather than the spectacle of new spatio-temporal relations. In a sense they seem to lack the most vital juncture, that with the present, the immediate perceived present. Their idea necessitates the Impressionist technique.

Read in its own original context of 1876, 'The Impressionists and Edouard Manet' shows a familiarity and engagement with matters central to the contemporary debate in painting and it combines this with a capacity to manipulate the latest technical ideas. This is clarified, for example when the text is read against critics such as Zola,[13] Antonin Proust[14] and Duret.[15] It goes beyond them in the way it seeks to synthesise developments in ideas and techniques in a complex definition of 'open-air' painting and the Japanese perspective as a significant moment in Western tradition, and in its anticipation of what was to follow. Furthermore it appears to understand Manet's controversial use of specific paintings as sources to be an historical strategy (otherwise sometimes called plagiariam or incompetence!)[16] in the theoretical framework of Michelet and Thoré'. Mallarmé's argument concerning the democratic nature of Impressionism and the position of French art in the European tradition is a function of this, although it remains implicit very largely. Both he and Manet were politically evasive, tending to suppress the relationships between ideological and formal questions so that such relationships emerge as transformations.

Read in the context of the rest of Mallarmé's critical writing, 'The Impressionists and Edouard Manet' is extended and it also qualifies his theory of poetry as well as of painting. It is much more developed than the better-known 'Le Jury de Peinture pour 1874 et M. Manet' which compares in scope as well as matter with his essays 'L'Art pour Tous', 'Catholicisme' and 'Étalages', and articles on the audience and the public. The closeness of 'The Impressionists and Edouard Manet' to 'Crise de Vers' in scope and structure integrates it on a fundamental level with Mallarmé's evolving theories of language. 'Crise de Vers' is composed of fragments written and published over at least ten years, and it forms part of his most substantial prose criticism and theory. Written in 1876, ten years earlier than the first published part of 'Crise de Vers', Mallarmé's analysis of the historical developments in painting is not simply a parallel, but is essentially and historically inseparable from his own experimentation with written language. Around this time Mallarmé published 'L'Après-Midi d'un Faune' (1876), with Manet's illustrations and the prose-poems 'Le Démon de l'Analogie' and 'Un Spectacle Interrompu', (published in 1874 and 1875 respectively) both written in 1864, like the first, very different drafts of 'L'Après-Midi d'un Faune'. These texts are a radical departure from the earliest poems and prose-poems and form part of the developments leading ultimately to 'Un Coup de Dés' which Mallarmé explicitly presented in his preface to that poem as a summarising form synthesising what amounts to a new genre incorporating *vers libre*, the prose-poem, music and visually controlled reading. It is the articulation of the same new 'problematic of the imaginary' as Impressionism. Mallarmé's terms are 'subdivisions prismatiques de l'idée', 'sujets d'imagination pure et complexe ou intellect' (455–6) and the achievement of the poem is much more than synaesthesia or the *Gesamtkunstwerk*, and, in the end, qualitatively different from them.

This provides a way of reading Mallarmé's innovations, including the 'espacement de lecture' of 'Un Coup de Dés', and those in painting, as part of the same problematic, and as a continuing process. Leaving aside the musical dimension, there seems to be a basic connection between this problematic as a fundamental change and the rapprochement of language and visual expression.

This is confirmed by his other writing on painting, such as *Le 10 o'Clock de M. Whistler* (a translation of Whistler's lecture), the Preface to Berthe Morisot's posthumous exhibition and certain of the shorter prose sketches and poems. Recognising the connection allows closer access to the whole network into which these ideas are inserted – through Whistler to England, the Pre-Raphaelites, the Aesthetic movement, and in France to Fantin-Latour, Courbet, Degas; through Redon to Les XX in Belgium, to Gauguin and the Post-Impressionists as well as what we regard as 'mainstream' Impressionism – Morisot, Monet and Renoir. This is not to say that Mallarmé is some kind of prime mover or pivot, on whom this wealth of new ideas is centered. On the contrary, I would counter that kind of reading which, by separating him off as the leader, in advance of his time, has tended to render his meanings obscure when they need not be. Worse, such a reading is symptomatic of the type of overall view which sees great individuals and separate movements without theorising that plurality either by trying to account for it or by asking what effect a complex set of inter-relationships has on meaning. In Barthes's words, 'ce que la modernité donne à lire dans la pluralité de ses écritures, c'est l'impasse de sa propre Histoire'.[17]

It has become difficult to see past categories and labels such as those I have just listed, particularly as received art-historical practice all too often perpetuates them, regardless of whether they were adopted by the artists themselves (Les XX), or were invented at the time (Impressionism), or were attached later (Post-Impressionism). The breadth needed to make sense of the last term was highlighted by the 1980 Royal Academy exhibition, for example, which ranged all over Western Europe and included painters without whom no 'Symbolist' exhibition would be complete. In terms of individual painters whose work was innovative and experimental – Manet or Gauguin, for example – one is forced to speak of 'Impressionist phases'. The question of naming is no mere quibble over terminology because the labels come to establish a framework within which it is difficult to discern other comparisons or establish an intertextuality outside its reference points. Recognising the full implications of such restrictive effects locates a major problem in beginning to understand the range of Mallarmé's analysis in 'The Impressionists and Edouard Manet', both in art-historical terms and in relation to his own thought, and also has a bearing on how 'obscurities' in Mallarmé and Manet were perceived, their 'illisibilité'.

In a short chapter entitled 'La Fin de l'Impressionisme', Francastel[18] outlined an argument for an analysis of Impressionism which differs from the general view.

Francastel's argument is relevant to the present case in two ways in particular. First it is a succinct critique of art-history as merely 'chronicle' and of the ways in which this affects our grasp of the relative importance of developments, tending to level out every change or innovation. And second, it is a clear, if schematic, definition of Impressionism and the way it specifically has been reduced by this process.

Francastel attacks the idea implicit in what have since been called '-ismatic' histories of nineteenth- and twentieth-century art: that all developments which followed Impressionism were comparable to it in type and importance. Impressionism is thus made to appear largely as a method for projecting signs from a transparent Nature onto two-dimensional canvas, a 'mode' on the one hand, a 'movement' on the other. What this obscures, Francastel argues, is that Impressionism was a formulation of a 'new problematic of the imaginary' and of 'new signifying relations of culture', both of which may be revealed by starting with a redefinition which takes acount of its socio-historic generation, as a product of modern culture. This is clearly not the place for such a project to be elaborated. But the need for it is a further indication of the extent and intricacy of the barriers to a full reading of 'The Impressionists and Edouard Manet'. The difficulty compounds the problem of understanding and describing the relationships and force-fields between written and painted texts and between literature and painting.

Critical metalanguage[19] has therefore evolved in such a way as to render 'Impressionism' and 'Symbolism' in poetry and painting either meaningless or misleading and to make it hard to be precise when transferring the terms between verbal and visual signs. It might be easy to accept, for example, Valéry's account of Impressionism and – another awkward term – 'absolute' poetry as manifestations of the same 'advent of pure sensibility' in that both somehow surpassed the Romantic notion of Imagination and the Realist version of Truth, and to understand up to a point that advances were brought about by the one in the search of optical pleasure, and by the other, under the influence of music, in the analysis of the power of the word itself. But his historical point requires that we include all current movements:

La poésie absolue, entrevue par Mallarmé, et l'Impressionisme à l'état naissant, l'une se référant à la source même de toute expression, l'autre ne retenant des choses et des êtres que leur dépendance de la lumière, ont un rapport plus étroit et plus significatif que celui d'une coincidence chronologique.[20]

Like Francastel, Valéry points out a vital connection, while taking his arguments to this point little further. The problems are recurrent and will remain unresolved while the old analytic framework endures.

Alongside Valéry's remarks may be placed further extracts from 'Crise de Vers' and also from one of the principal *vers-libristes*, Laforgue, whose essays on painting are analytic and attempt to delineate the transformations between art forms. Laforgue's texts are more explicitly, and less critically, expressed in Wagnerian terms and are more like Baudelaire than Mallarmé in this respect. They therefore supply a further contextual dimension, since as is well known Wagner served as a focus for many ideas then in debate.

The following passages are from 'Crise de Vers':

mon sens regrette que le discours défaille à exprimer les objets par des touches y répondant en coloris ou allure, lesquelles existent dans l'instrument de la voix, parmi les langages et quelquefois chez un.

Ouir l'indiscutable rayon – comme des traits dorent et déchirent un méandre de mélodies: où la Musique rejoint le Vers pour former, depuis Wagner, la Poésie.

Abolie la prétention . . . d'inclure au papier subtil du volume autre chose que par exemple l'horreur de la forêt, ou le tonnerre muet épars au feuillage. . . . [les mots] s'allument de reflects réciproques comme une virtuelle trainée de feux sur des pierreries, remplaçant la respiration perceptible en l'ancien souffle lyrique ou la direction personnelle enthousiaste de la phrase. (364, 5, 6.)

In the following passage Laforgue moves easily between Impressionism, Wagner and Symbolism, using the forest metaphor, which resonates from Baudelaire's 'Correspondances' and Mallarmé's 'Hérodiade', less obliquely than Mallarmé in the passage just quoted from 'Crise de Vers'. Mallarmé's shift from the forest itself to transferring to the page the horror and the silent thunder of the leaves allows the reader to slide between the leaves of the book and those of the trees, calling attention to the process of his written thought.

Though there is agreement in ideas, there is no such Impressionist reflexivity in the Laforgue:

tout est obtenu par mille touches menues dansantes en tous sens comme des pailles de couleurs – en concurrence vitale pour l'impression de l'ensemble. Plus de melodie isolée, le tout est une symphonie qui est la voix vivante et variante, comme les voix de la forêt de Wagner en concurrance vitale pour la grande voix de la forêt comme l'Inconsciente, loi du monde, est la grande voix mélodique, résultante de la symphonie des consciences des races et d'individus. Tel est le principe de l'école du plein-air impressioniste. Et l'œil du maître sera celui qui discernera et rendra des dégradations, les décompositions les plus sensibles, cela sur une simple toile plane. Ce principe a été, non systématiquement, mais par génie, appliqué en poésie et dans le roman chez nous.[21]

Laforgue identifies the fragmented and re-integrated touches of colour in Impressionism with the merging of the individual consciousness in collective unconscious and furthers this identification as a highly sophisticated manoeuvre through which the civilised artist regains the clarity of perception peculiar to primitive vision. (Mallarmé's observations about the democracy of Impressionism, its capacity to see with the eyes of the people and of Nature, may be recalled here.) By enabling the artist to forget 'les illusions tactiles et sa commode langue morte' (an example would be rejecting illusionist rendering of volumes, and flattening surfaces) the Impressionist vision, according to Laforgue, was most highly evolved in its discernment of reality. Instead of translating a single version of the represented subject (or, one might add, a single version of the mind, as in surrealism) into paint, what is attended to is the mobile texture of undirected thinking and perceiving – 'la réalité dans l'atmosphère vivante des formes, décomposée, réfractée, réfléchie [to the English reader, reflected, thought] par les êtres et les choses, en incessantes variations'.[22] Light and sound both initiate and erase painted and spoken thought-process, and Mallarmé extends ink and written thought, to include all active traces. A time-process mental function is thus in his account represented by the broken brushmark of Impressionism, which is expressive in this autonomous sense rather than 'Expressionist' – it is qualitatively different from the Expressionist, since it tends to be entropic.[23]

Mallarmé's Impressionism is a refined perception, a heightened sense of discontinuities, focusing the points of transition between the inaccessible unconscious and the conscious, while signifying the conjunction of the unconscious with sense-impressions and the sharing of innate unexpressed 'knowledge' revealing structures affecting perception and thought. Through it we might begin to explore the 'new problematic of the imaginary' which Francastel points towards, because it offers a coherent basis for analysis of 'Symbolism', 'Impressionism', 'Post-Impressionism' and, including 'Cubism', as differing movements within the 'new signifying relations of culture'. In technique, verbal shifts and syntactic structures alter in accordance with comparable principles with the distortions in line, scale and perspective consequent on Impressionist foregrounding of the depiction of light, and the processes thereby initiated. If later Impressionism seems to be a cul-de-sac – a view which is widely held – it is because it lost sight of some of its fundamental discoveries, becoming partial, and this is a reduction criticism has tended to perpetuate. In 1876, Mallarmé saw in Manet the whole beginning.

Mallarmé's terms of reference include the political as defined by Kristeva in the following quotation. Kristeva refers to the passage at the end of 'The Impressionists and Edouard Manet' where Mallarmé stresses the 'radical and democratic' nature of Impressionism, and its significance as on a par with the 'social fact' of greater political freedom (84).

Saisir l'aspect passager – tel est le but qui rapproche par exemple un parti (visant a traduire le *procès* dans les *institutions* établies) et l'impressionisme (qui ramène le procès inconnu jusque dans la *toile*); par cette tendance, précisément, l'impressionisme, et toute pratique d'avant-garde sans doute s'apparente au surgissement sur la scène politique (donc dans les 'structures') de ce qui en est le portent mobile, à savoir le *peuple*; et Mallarmé de comparer le mouvement impressioniste à 'la participation du peuple jusqu'ici ignoré de la vie politique en France'.[24]

In his inclusive definition of Impressionism, Mallarmé embraces all aspects both of Manet (his allusions and experiments with historical technique) and of non-Impressionist painters. His remarks about Impressionism and politics indicate a structure which locates the art of that precise historical moment (1876) in a continuum implicating the past and the future.

For example, Mallarmé affirms that Impressionism 'is the principal and real movement of contemporary painting. The only one? No; since other talents have been devoted to illustrate some particular phrase [sic] or period of bygone art; among these we must class such artists as Moreau, Puvis de Chavannes, etc.' (83–4). Mallarmé contrasts the visionary art of the past with the simplicity of the present, the former as the vision of 'kings and gods', with dominion over the multitude, the latter as belonging to that multitude and with the aim of speaking directly to the future. The comparison with the art of 'the far dream ages of mankind' is apt; it is a reclaiming of transcendent and visionary experience for the depiction of the ordinary, a reinsertion of mythic experience as process into contemporary history.

In order to understand the treatment of myth in these texts the reader cannot simply peel off a layer or re-interpret signs in order to recover the lost world. The Renaissance conception of myth as belonging to a distinct historical epoch, to be contemplated with nostalgia, appears as an ironic counterpoint to the powerfully present, uncompromisingly diffuse mythic potential glimpsed in Mallarmé.

> Mes bouquins refermés sur le nom de Paphos,
> Il m'amuse d'élire avec le seul génie
> Une ruine . . .   (76)

Mallarmé equally differentiated his democratic and formal exploration from the widely influential Wagnerian recreation of a great theatrical, nationalist legend, which revived the old myths without radically remaking them. The thematic texture of many of Mallarmé's poems and his essays analysing ritual, the theatre, and collective experience may indeed use Wagnerian vocabulary at times, but his epistemology relates to it as Copernican astronomy to Ptolemaic.

Reading Mallarmé requires some reinsertion of mythic thought into our account of cognitive process, which means that those areas of experience designated as 'mythopoeic' should be understood in terms which do not oppose them to logic. In anthropology Lévi-Strauss pointed out the limitation of denying 'to "primitive mentality" its cognitive character'. This had initially been conceded to it, before it was 'cast back entirely into the realm of affectivity'. To restate the problem in these terms is important because in so doing he does not separate out as incomprehensible one part of experience; while recognising that the accessibility of mythic thought is indirect, Lévi-Strauss insists that it is not separate. There are no such things as 'ineffable or untranslatable cognitive data'. 'Mystère' exists; I am not saying that at any time everything is accessible. It is the translation that becomes important.

The question is raised in Mallarmé's remarks about music, where he allows his text movement between individual expression and historical moment and collective experience, expressed in rapid shifts between levels of generality, as in the whole of the final section of 'Crise de Vers', or in his essay on Wagner. Like myth, music is not consigned to the realm of affectivity, 'car, ce n'est pas de sonorités élémentaires par les cuivres, les cordes, les bois, indéniablement mais de l'intellectuelle parole à son apogée que doit avec plénitude et évidence, résulter, en tant que l'ensemble des rapports existant dans tout, la Musique' (367–8). Music is also the art in which semiosis is introverted, where the questions of form and representation are most clearly to be seen as interdependent.

The critical problems raised by Mallarmé's idea of 'music' would seem to be: how do we read apparently self-enclosed texts both on the level of myth and of social reality? How does the reality of society come to be represented mentally? Texts which foreground their own creative process approach such transformations as they occur and are reproduced. In so doing, they concern power and the relation of the law to entry into culture:

> Ne faut il pas songer à l'étrange origine
> Aux nourritures plus souples dans le futur
> Et si peut-être un passé nous incline.   (Edith Boissonas. 'Accalmie')

3

SELF SIGN WORLD

— Chacun son tour, il est temps que je m'émancipe,
Irradiant des Limbes mon inédit type!

Jules Laforgue. 'Complainte du foetus de Poète'

The participation of a hitherto ignored people in the political life of France is a social fact
that will honour the whole of the close of the nineteenth century . . .
. . . today the multitude demands to see with its own eyes.

Mallarmé. 'The Impressionists and Edouard Manet'

In this chapter I shall concentrate on form. I shall examine written and painted texts
together in order to outline how they initiate meaning, from the zero point (between
meanings or between meaning and non-meaning) or from the moment of change
between visual and aural signs. I want to focus on this area because both types of
signification are present in written and painted texts, but with crucial differences.
Even the obvious one, that written texts use words while many painted texts do not,
is not simple to describe in such a way as to make it useful in analysing them together.
A certain amount of technical vocabulary (deriving from linguistics) is necessary and
I have tried to be as clear as possible in using it. Furthermore, an important strand in
the argument concerns mental process and perception. There is therefore a second,
psychoanalytic vocabulary, which I shall use in conjunction with the first.

In the movements within and between texts tensions are set up, but the final term
which might complete meaning is refused so that no place in socially instituted
exchange is assigned to the signified. The transformations appear as primal phanta-
sies which lead back to the body from which they derive – the somatic self and the
language-body – and are narcissistic in that their rebound from culture seems to defy
the idea that exchange is the *a priori* condition governing the generation of meaning.
Mallarmé defends the resultant difficulty in 'Le Mystère dans les Lettres':

Si, tout de même, n'inquiétait je ne sais quel miroitement, en dessous, peu séparable de la surface
concédée à la rétine – il attire le soupçon: les malins, entre le public, réclament de couper court, opinent,
avec serieux, que, juste, la teneur est inintelligible.   (382)

Signs are necessary to the self-relation, internally, before exchange. The self-referring meanings reflecting off each other in this mirroring process are not unconscious, pathological or inarticulate, but are deflected across forms of articulation as in 'Un Coup de Dés':

> dans ces parages
> ['séparage'][1]
>
> du vague
>
> en quoi toute réalité se dissout   (475)

What can be learnt from the tensions thus set up between the Subject as an individual and as functioning in a specific historical and social location, moving through cultural transactions which remake the myths embodied in signs?

Valéry's definition of myth cited in Littré is as follows: 'Mythe est le nom de tout ce qui n'existe et ne subsiste qu'ayant la parole pour cause.' One reading of this is that myth is a linguistic phenomenon, the name of that which is sustained by speech. Of necessity it concerns language, and language in its diachronic axis. It was and is initiated by speech, a reflexive and potential, inclusive area predicated on the spoken without excluding the written. As a specific message, the statement that myth is 'le nom' with 'la parole' as its cause is a duplex type. It is an autonymous (sic) mode,[2] a message referring to the code. Valéry's syntax implies the relation between myth and duplex language functions.

In any semiotic event the message and the code are capable of working in two ways at once, as both tool and artefact. That is, they may be utilised and referred to, as implied for example in Barthes's model of myth as metalanguage and mode of representation as language–object.[3] A sign in the latter becomes a signifier in the former, mythic language. More specifically, Jakobson distinguishes four particular structures which always function in this duplex way as tool and artefact. They are further divided into two kinds of circularity (message referring to message, code to code) and two kinds of overlapping (message referring to code, code to message). But in neither of these is it possible to take account of the subject as active in the process, since they describe simply the semiotic event within the system.

The shifter[4] is of particular interest in this context, since it also combines the properties of two types of sign – the index and the symbol. It plays an important part in language acquisition and may therefore be expected to assume a role in semantic and formal innovation.

The meaning of the shifter cannot be defined within the code alone, but only with reference to the message. The two types of sign which it combines (the index and the symbol) maintain an existential and a conventional relation respectively with the signified. An index is not necessarily verbal or artificial: the pointing finger is the best known example. This combination of an existential relation with one defined by the language or semiotic system offers a particular insight into the way the historical subject may be seen as implicated in the language. The possibility of a signifier whose relation to the signified at both levels (of object–language and metalanguage) may be both arbitrary and necessary is therefore open, allowing immensely rich generative potential in the resultant tension between speaking Subject, code and specific message.

The personal pronoun is a shifter, an indexical symbol, one which focuses the overlap between code and message on the Subject. The relation between a semiotic sequence in any language-code and the person uttering it is conventional, that of the symbol. 'I' on the page has no necessary association with me, only with 'the one who utters' – that is with the sender of a message, a semiotic function. The sender however, in reflexive self-designation, bears an existential relation to the message, and is thus implicated in it, in language and in body, or mind, or self-in-relation to language, or in any combination of these, according to the specific message.

The shifter is a duplex structure which, together with the three others implicating message and code, is prominent in Mallarmé's 'L'Après-Midi d'un Faune'. 'Aimai-je un rêve?', a rhetorical question, perhaps, with the Faune addressing itself. The poem is headed 'Le Faune'; later 'Faune' is used as a proper noun ('Faune, l'illusion s'échappe des yeux bleus'), and in this 'Faune' is an example of the code referring to the code. 'Faune' is anyone so called. Without reference to the code it has no general meaning. The two functions of 'Faune' are structurally related in the poem since they are applied to the same persona, the sender of the message.

But the sender, by addressing itself, is sometimes the receiver. The first main section following 'Réfléchissons . . .' compounds the problematic relations of the sender(s) and receiver(s), and thus the status of the message. The Faune is addressed as 'tu' and as 'Faune'. The interjection 'Que non!' is then unclear in function, since it might equally introduce a reply from another speaker or the continuation of an interior monologue. 'Je' does not recur until the next section when it is inside inverted commas. In reported speech, the duplex structure is that of message referring to message. Furthermore, these are preceded by 'CONTEZ', in grammatical and typographical distinction from 'Réfléchissons'. ('Contez', second person, either plural or more ceremonious than the earlier 'tu'.) The entire poem is structured on interpreting its own words and sentences, and is in this sense 'autonymous', a message constantly referring to its code. The autonymous is a pervasive mode in Mallarmé, which also operates at the lexical level.

The existential relation in this poem between the Subject and the sign 'I', then, implies the Subject without fixing it. To illustrate this with reference to an object with a general meaning outside the language-event, we may take the flute intermittently played by the Faune, a twin reed, doubled like the nymphs, and divided like the Faune's physical form:

> Le jonc vaste et jumeau dont sous l'azur on joue:
> Qui, détournant à soi le trouble de la joue,
> Rêve, dans un solo long, que nous amusions
> La beauté d'alentour par des confusions
> Fausses entre elle-même et notre chant crédule;
> . . .

Tâche donc, instrument des fuites, ô maligne
Syrinx, de refleurir aux lacs où tu m'attends!

The homophonic rhyme of the first couplet proposes differing linguistic registers enacting the existential. Thus, through the reed the physical action of the cheek and of the emotion, both signified by 'trouble', become music, are played. The verb becomes the noun. The projection of an internal event into the outside world is indicated both semantically and syntactially. 'On joue' is already a form of self-distancing for the first person. By the end of the section, it is the inanimate flute which has the full status in language as a Subject. 'Syrinx', a proper noun, is addressed by the 'je'.

This section begins with a reference to the story of Pan and Syrinx in which, according to Ovid, the nymph, in order to escape the god was turned into a bunch of reeds at the moment he caught her. In the poem, the metamorphosis is never complete, the level on which the cultural transformations from Ovid through his translators affect the moment of the poem is open-ended.

In Manet, structures which focus on the message and code in the same way also predominate in a large number of paintings. The same is true of much of the best painting of the period overall. *Un Déjeuner sur l'Herbe* (fig. 8) for example, on this structural level relates closely to 'L'Après-Midi d'un Faune', of which more will be said below. Manet's inclusion of himself in a composite text like *La Pêche*,[5] and his self-quotation as in *Le Vieux Musicien* (fig. 31), similarly made up of a collection of elements taken from other paintings, includes the sender of his own message with historical figures and carriers of meaning. Like Manet, Redon quotes and requotes himself and the texts out of which he constructs his own intertextuality. Like the Faune's reported speech, its own memories, such repetitions are forms of 'represented discourse', displaced or relayed across the event.

In spatial terms, the division of the picture space, as in Redon's *À l'horizon l'ange des Certitudes, et dans un ciel sombre, un regard intérrogateur* (fig. 32), may set part of the text in such a relation to the rest that it functions autonomously. This is particularly the case when the division is reinforced representationally, as in Gauguin's *D'où venons-nous, que sommes-nous, où allons-nous?* (fig. 33). In this painting, the predominating blue of the composition is layered with the orange background of the linguistic message at the top two corners. The blue sky-area then declares itself as a fictional space constructed by the painted narrative. The clearest examples of this device in Manet are in his portraits of the two writers, Astruc and Zola. In the first, the sitter is placed beside a mirror which reflects a scene occupying the space which as spectator, or receiver, we would share with the painter, or sender – that is, in front of the painting. The device is neither new nor especially rare in itself, although its use here is ambiguous. It becomes more complex in relation to similar divisions in *Olympia* (fig. 71), in the Zola portrait where the mirror is replaced by paintings, some of which share the same frame, or in paintings in which there is a barrier of some sort – the railings of *Le Chemin de Fer* (fig. 16) or *Le Balcon*, (fig. 13), for example.

31   Manet, *Le Vieux Musicien*, 1862

32   Redon, À *l'horizon l'ange des Certitudes, et dans un ciel sombre, un regard intérrogateur*, 1882

33   Gauguin, *D'où venons-nous, que sommes nous, où allons-nous*, 1897

34   Manet, *Un Bar aux Folies Bergères*, 1882

36 Whistler, *Symphony in White No.2:
The Little White Girl*, 1864

35 Whistler, *Symphony in White No.1:
The White Girl*, 1862

37 Whistler, *Symphony in White No.3*, 1865/7

A most striking example of this autonymous mode is *Un Bar aux Folies Bergères* (fig. 34) which, like *D'où venons-nous, que sommes-nous, où allons-nous?* uses the complementaries blue and orange to effect a stable but polarised colour code,[6] in which a transaction is represented between a man and a woman. There is a barrier at the foot of the painting and across the middle, with a partial barrier in between. The manner in which the painting's spatial construction is perceived depends crucially on how these barriers are read. Their repetition is passively reinforced by the two vertical columns, dividers splitting the top quarter with their white discs or lights. Several readings are suggested, left incomplete and mutually incompatible, as long as the painting is assumed to be a unitary sign.

If, however, like 'L'Après-Midi d'un Faune', it is read as complex and tending towards iconicity, this structure is comprehensible in cognitive terms. After the model of the shifter, let us propose in addition to the conventional relations an existential relation with the represented object. Like 'Un Coup de Dés' in Valéry's formulation, the painting is 'the figure of a thought'. As we have seen above, its structure may incorporate a temporal element, in which case the spatial discontinuities appear rather as temporal progression, the inconsistencies and repetitions in vertical and horizontal structures (the bar and the balcony, the lights and the columns) as registering peripheral vision. This may readily be seen in *D'où venons-nous* . . . (fig. 33). It is a mode which need not be restricted to one text; in Whistler the *Symphonies in White* build up a multiplex sign internally and in series.

The first of these, *Symphony in White No. 1. The White Girl* (fig. 35) is spatially limited by the curtain, isolating the figure. In the second, (fig. 36)[7] which repeats many of the features of the first, the lower two thirds are contained by the white fireplace and the figure itself, while the reflected face with the painted seascape behind it occupies a space without restriction which is also the assumed location of the spectator or receiver. The third of the series (fig. 37) is once more enclosed but contains two figures with the same accessories of flowers and fan and white interior. What they signify remains open. They propose a relation, spatialise the whiteness.

The theatricality of these texts, including 'L'Après-Midi d'un Faune', which was written for theatrical presentation, is more than a certain 'staginess'; the balcony in *Un Bar aux Folies Bergères* (fig. 34) with its audience in a dislocated paraxial space is not unitary in semiotic function, though it is specific. Apart from the spatio-temporal movement introduced by the inclusion of more than one internal space in the painting, as already indicated, the bodies and the objects are arranged on display as on stage, a type of ostension.[8] In the theatre people act as signifiers of people as signifieds – the relation of the actor to the persona. The scenery, or indeed any arrangement of displayed objects, may use the same form of communication as for example the pile of clothes in *Un Déjeuner sur l'Herbe* (fig. 8) or the props in the *Frontispiece* to Manet's etchings, *Collection de Huit Eaux-Fortes* (fig. 38). As a filmic trope, furthermore, this layering of signification may act as a close non-verbal equivalent to dialogue (or monologue).

38   Manet, frontispiece to *Collection de Huit Eaux-Fortes*, 1862

As a form of signification, ostension is most apparent in Mallarmé in the prose-poems and in 'Igitur'. 'Le Démon de l'Analogie' implicates language in this by projecting the empty sound-sequence[9] and the experiential levels in several ways:

'La phrase revint, virtuelle, dégagée d'une chute antérieure de plume ou de rameau, dorénavant à travers la voix entendue, jusqu'à ce qu'enfin elle s'articula seule, vivant de sa personnalité.' (272–3)

Towards the end of the text the wing, the chord of the (vocal) instrument and the defunct modes of thought to which the first person narrator ascribes the meaningless fragment are made concretely manifest in the window display. Like Dupin's walk through the streets at the beginning of Poe's 'The Murders in the Rue Morgue', the analytic method is enacted in the subject's interaction with the material world-as-presented. The method subsists in the interaction and cannot be restated. The relationship between the speaker and the language is, as it were, equalised. Projected outwards, the subject can then observe itself and language, a form of self-creation in articulation.[10] This may take many forms and may operate at the level of the individual speaker and text or as in intertextual function. In the following passage from 'L'Action Restreinte' Mallarmé's 'spirituel histrion' meets its own gaze in a hallucinatory theatrical representation:

L'écrivain, de ses maux, dragons qu'il a choyés, ou d'une allégresse, doit s'instituer, au texte, le spirituel histrion.

Plancher, lustre, obnubilation des tissus et liquéfaction de miroirs, en l'ordre réel, jusqu'aux bonds excessifs de notre forme gazée autour d'un arrêt, sur pied, de la virile stature, un Lieu se présente, scène, majoration devant tous de spectacle de Soi; là, en raison des intermédiaires de la lumière, de la chair et des rires le sacrifice qu'y fait, relativement à sa personnalité, l'inspirateur, aboutit complet ou c'est, dans une resurrection étrangère, fini de celui-ci: de qui le verbe répercuté et vain désormais s'exhale par la chimère orchestrale.

Une salle, il se célèbre, anonyme, dans le héros. (370–371)

In this passage, to which I shall return, may be recognised both the immediacy of simultaneous synthesis[11] and the fragmentary perceptions of less differentiated vision[12] and thought that precede it. There are again heterogeneous levels of perception running through the passage as in the prose-poem. These subsist in the objects named, the variable presence of the writer as sender and receiver of the message and the interchangeability of words and things.

In *D'où venons-nous . . .* (fig. 33) and the *Symphony in White* series (figs. 35–37), which I have already mentioned, the verbal element is more active in signification than a tautologous 'title'. But it is not equal with the visual in generating meaning. Redon's lithographic series, however, set verbal and visual codes in productive relation to each other, with neither given priority. In this they are already classifiable as autonymous in mode, because whenever words are used to elucidate signs they constitute a message referring to the code. The same is true of translation, and the transfer from written to painted or lithographic sign is intersemiotic translation. Redon exploits the potential of word and image referring to each other. For example, in the fourth of his series *À Edgar Poe*, the verbal component is *À l'horizon l'ange des Certitudes, et dans un ciel sombre, un regard intérrogateur* (fig. 32). As a semiotic event this title is already complex; in addition to its position relative to the lithograph, it is fourth in a series of six, each of which bears a varying relation to the work of Poe, a writer in another language. Reference to Poe in 1882 in France connoted reference to Baudelaire as translator of his tales and to a more restricted but significant extent, to Mallarmé and to Manet's illustrated translation of 'The Raven' (1875). It has also been suggested by Sandström that the lithograph derives from Durer's *Melencolia I*, which is a rebus. Finally, the words are by Redon, though they were taken to be quotations from Poe – just as, for example, the words of his Flaubert series are quotations from the 'original'.

Redon's practice in relating the verbal component of his lithographic albums to the image and to the sequence is variable. Where the words come from pre-existing works – Flaubert, Bulwer-Lytton, Baudelaire – they are combined into a complex sign, not juxtaposed as 'illustration': 'C'est un mot à trouver: je ne vois que ceux de transmission, d'interprétation.'[13] Using Barthes's terms, they may be said to function as a relay-text.[14] When the words were conceived as titles, they were to introduce a further source of meaning. 'Le titre n'est justifié que lorsqu'il est vague, indéterminé, et visant même confusément à l'equivoque.'[15] Images and words are both elements in an overall syntagm[16] realising the message at a level outside that of the immediate verbal or visual 'frame'. Diegesis – the advancing of both action and the conveying of information necessary to the message – may be now in the image, now in the text, making for an initially extremely costly, but very dense mode of signification. 'Costly', that is to say, in terms of the economy of the work (again in Barthes's adaptation of, in this case, Freudian terms), the foci and quantity of effort required to decode the message.

In the present example of the fourth of the Poe series, something of this initially costly mode has already been outlined at the contextual level. The sign is made up of a layered, diffuse but coherent complex of signifiers within which it works to generate meaning. It does not represent either them, or reality, or an idea. Similarly the verbal and visual component of the sign force attention to their formal relation. The words convey little additional information; they appear tautologous in this case, since they also offer no purely linguistic mode, such as a proposition or instruction, to assist or extend the visual sign. Redon's theory implies that the linguistic signifiers should not propose or instruct, but rather should set up a tension between them and the visual signifiers, impeding access to unitary or simple meaning. This also operates in Mallarmé in terms of the interaction of concrete, figurative and abstract image-making, especially in 'Un Coup de Dés'. Here the title is both set in the conventional place at the beginning of the text and inserted into it, thus both working as anchor and as relay. Mallarmé describes the process as:

un jet de grandeur, de pensée ou d'émoi, considérable, phrase poursuivie, en gros caractère, une ligne par page à emplacement gradué, ne maintiendrait-il le lecteur en haleine, la durée du livre, avec appel à sa puissance d'enthousiasme; autour, menus, des groupes, secondairement d'après leur importance, explicatifs ou dérivés – un semis de fioritures.   'Le Livre, Instrument Spirituel'. (381)

The drive of these texts is towards iconicity, the invention of signs in which the relation between signifier and signified is necessary, not arbitrary. The inevitable gap between drive and invention itself has a positive function: each time it is differently formed. The same is true of their deliberate, seemingly perverse refusal of clarity. Taken as a moving formation they cross and recross the limits of sense and, let it be stressed, of form. The words in Mallarmé mobilise a kind of scansion which mimics both the apprehension of spoken language and of painting, where information is gleaned successively, across time, but then reforms as a present totality which is decoded by means of 'simultaneous synthesis'. This process is exactly described, for example, in Mallarmé's Preface to 'Un Coup de Dés':

cette distance copiée qui mentalement sépare des groupes de mots ou les mots entre eux, semble d'accélérer tantôt et de ralentir le mouvement, le scandant, l'intimant même selon une vision simultanée de la Page.

Simultaneous synthesis functions in 'Un Coup de Dés' through spatial manipulation as an historical principle from 'l'antique vers' to 'l'avenir qui sortira d'ici' (456).

The striking achievement of 'Un Coup de Dés', in this respect is that it transfers the temporal characteristic of spoken language on to the page, where it is possible both to exploit the spatial character of the visual sign *and* to preserve the whole message. In so doing the text transgresses the fundamental difference between visual and aural signs and their perception. That is to say, when we look at a visual sign we go through a process which involves successive perceptual acts followed by simultaneous synthesis in which we grasp the message in its totality – and then still have all parts of the process before us. This is not true of the spoken message because when synthesis is reached, the phonemes have ceased to exist and, like after-images, become abridged reminiscences. This alters the nature of the semiotic event and affects memory. As in 'Prose pour des Esseintes', apperception is sudden, intense, appearing to present itself out of some occult, closed or impenetrable source, call it unconscious or unintelligible:

> Hyperbole! de ma mémoire
> Triomphalement ne sais-tu
> Te lever, aujourd'hui grimoire
> Dans un livre de fer vêtu. (55)

As in Impressionism, a hitherto internal perceptual fact is externalised and presented to the senses, initiating a definitive change in thought and signifying processes. It is a dialogue between internal and external realities, such as played upon in 'L'Après-Midi d'un Faune', a dialogue which both begins and ends with references outside its enacted time-space.

Transgressive movements may affect formal structures in different ways. The depiction of the perceptual act of interpreting light at the moment it strikes the retina is not an isolated, merely passive and technical trick. It is an altered spatio-temporal signification, which operates at a pre-logical cognitive level. The same is true of Manet's spatial distortions and the compositional features both in his work and in 'Symbolist' paintings (by Gauguin, Redon or Seurat, for example) characterised as 'dream-like'. Rather than dream in the negative sense of withdrawal from the waking state or from external reality, such texts constitute a mode whereby the reality principle is extended. That is, their drive is towards incorporating repressed, forgotten and transgressive functions into consciousness – and, also, towards establishing a relation between the perceiving subject and reality which, as in the dream, is fluid and susceptible to alteration. As with wish-fulfilment in the dream-work, it allows the release of unpleasure and the reconciliation of the self and reality: 'l'air charge / De vue et non de vision' in the space glimpsed in 'Prose pour des Esseintes' (56).

Similarly in Redon, the serial form, the alternation in relay-function between verbal and visual components in the complex sign *and* the dislocated spatial construction open on to, and seek to structure, pre-syntactic levels of cognitive and emotive experience. The angel, to return to the example of the fourth in the Poe series (fig. 32), inhabits a segmented space which makes the sky appear like a flat plane or thin wall. The eye of the 'regard sombre' is subject to a perceptual oscillation according to the spectator's sense-making activity. If 'moon' is assigned as a signified, it appears as a part of the sphere formed by its light background, and floats before the dark sky. If, however, 'detail of face' is supplied, it recedes behind the sky – in this way all the elements may be inverted. If a message is assumed, to whom is it addressed? – to Poe, to the angel or to the spectator? Since the participants in the event are unclear, the status of the message is brought into question, and turned inwards. The speaking subject subsumes its surroundings in a reciprocal dissolution and reconstitution.

The same and other comparable features are present, as we have seen, in texts by Manet and Mallarmé. *Un Déjeuner sur l'Herbe* (fig. 8) and 'L'Après-Midi d'un Faune', for example, are similarly spatially transgressive, and furthermore express the same ironic delight, what Kristeva has called in Giotto the 'sublimated jouissance' of the liberated subject.[17] Or again in Manet's Frontispiece to the album of etchings (fig. 38), with Polichinelle bursting through the curtain-wall on to a stage set with the props of painting.

As with the forms of ostension described above, the spatial structures I have just described may be compared with the hallucinatory representation of the first part of the dream-work, where desire is realised, by replacing the wish with its factual expression.[18] The direction is from the thought to the perception. In this, logical relations are dissolved and replaced by those of a form of pictorial representation which enacts the thought in a different register from language. The processes of condensation, displacement and indirect representation in Freud's theory both of the dream and of the joke[19] are movements between registers of thought, feeling and perception directed towards primary processes. They by-pass censorship, evading both repression and the secondary revision of conscious thought.

These are all functions which open up the image to the differing generative possibilities of tropes or forms peculiar to varying types of presentation rather than re-presentation. Since the structure derives from the dedifferentiated level of the primary processes,[20] and since the organisational principles of any such formation is dynamic and derives from the *transference* of its raw material, affect[21] or relations (in logical or cognitive terms), no single direction, form or trope will predominate. The cognitive or referential function is certainly lowered, but not excluded, and will co-exist with elements which in its terms appear arbitrary. This sets up immense tensions within the work. If it were not the case that the relation to the real and to rational process is maintained the strangeness and intensity of impact – the disruptive capacity – would be much reduced. Dream and fantasy elements are familiar enough in all art; much less familiar is the structure of the mind's movements between the inner area, in which anything is possible, but incommunicable, to the outer. The manifest content would be much easier to deal with if it were irrelevant, or structured by chance, as in Dada. The question that becomes pressing is: what happens when the dream is asked to signify communicable matter?

In a paper 'A mythological parallel to a visual obsession', Freud refers to the occurrence of an image having a paronomasic connection with the word 'Patriarch'.[22] As an example of a transgressive movement initiated by the unconscious, and as an underlying image related to creativity and power at the deepest dedifferentiated level, it shows how verbal residues can affect visual perception. The way Freud explains the incident is equally illuminating. His patient was distressed by the appearance of an obsessive image of the naked lower part of the body, with arms and legs, but no head or upper part, the genitals not indicated and with facial features painted on the abdomen. This image entered his mind when his father came into the room, and it was accompanied with the word 'fatherarse'. The image is a further presentation of the word. Freud relates it to terracotta figures of Baubo, and the story about her making Demeter laugh by lifting up her dress to expose her body. The terracotta figures show the body of a woman, no head or breasts, with a face on the abdomen and the dress framing it like hair.

In this transformation, the image merges into that of the Medusa. All the variants of the image I have referred to are clearly to do with the presence or absence of male or female genitalia and the mitigation or control of terror. They include, but are not restricted to, castration in the sense of a general incapacity. The Medusa's power works through sight, through being seen, and so fear of her is associated with sight. Rather than inarticulate it is perhaps 'aposiopetic' – that is, it brings speech to a halt. The disappearance of the male organ, when it is not castration, is re-entry into the womb. The perception of the father as female is open to more than one reading. The site of pleasure and of fear, of creativity and sterility is the same. The image of Freud's patient, which he projected outwards on to the, as it were, externally perceived father, and saw, may be understood as the attempted resolution of his internalised and repressed feelings about his father's self as he perceived it, in contra-distinction to the way others did – a readjustment of internal and social self-in-language. As Freud suggests in the celebrated Schreber case,[23] the 'delusional formation' is the attempt of the psyche to reconstruct a reality which allows the release of unpleasure and the generation of pleasure. The vision, in other words, is not indicative of a withdrawal from reality, but an attempt at perceptual readjustment in order to allow pleasurable reconciliation of subjective truths with external fact.

The patriarch/fatherarse formation works as a condensation of both verbal and visual forbidden thoughts into a single sign. It begins with a direct relation between the verbal and visual sign, but in Freud's account, it moves off according to an abstract of the shape. In unpacking the sign, Freud reverses one of the metonymic movements by means of which elements in a dream become overdetermined. This is the importation of material in the dream-work through the connoted meanings of each part of a paranomasic function. Any such condensed word or image appears in the dream's manifest content as representing a nodal point. It can invest minor or trivial features with significance, thereby displacing them towards the centre, or into prominence, and other material initially present in the dream-thought to the periphery.

There is thus an overlap between primary and secondary material which may set up a chain-like but not merely linear movement. The synecdochic figures tend to overlap each with the other as well as with the main figure – making a dense and involute structure which is experienced as a ricochet, an implosive violence. It induces anxiety because it tends to overwhelm and constantly to re-form. The spaces of field painting, the light-effect of Impressionism, the disjunctions of Manet's perspectival distortions and of Mallarmé's syntax may all be experienced as menacing on at least one level, since they open up this dedifferentiated perception into which the ego may be threatened with incorporation. It is quick to defend itself and focus on the secondary which it can organise and defuse.

In the case of the 'patriarch/fatherarse' formation, if it were not in poor taste, the lexical and visual paranomasia would comprise rather a good joke. Indeed, the mythological analogue is funny and involves releasing Demeter's unpleasure with the sight of something related to the forbidden (concealed parts of her body which are, by visual connection, related to totemic representations of both fertility and death) and occasioning sudden laughter. Demeter was unhappy because her daughter had been abducted. Direct reference to either sexual material or death would thus be impossible for social reasons. But the surprise action shows to conscious perception a pre-conscious thought-shape, and after the pattern of joke-formation, bypasses secondary revision. Through such indirect modes of signification the texts can create in the receiver of the message a powerful impression of potential meaning. Analysing the movements of the text at this level in detail elucidates the thematic structures of works which claim status as psychic events. If, as Mallarmé said, poetic language is not secondary to events, then what is a metaphor? 'Le Livre, Instrument Spirituel' and 'Étalages', for example, are about 'le fait de la pensée' and language as giving access to mythopoeic levels, 'approchant d'un rite le composition typographique'. Where they are at their most innovatory and exciting, they focus on the transfer between thought-structures and sensory perceptions, and include that function which Freud indicated in the dreamwork which cannot be attributed to regression – that is, the change back into sensory images. They are visual images that present reality through visionary structures.

T. S. Eliot said of Dante's poetry that it was the product of a visual imagination which differed from that of a modern painter: 'it is visual in the sense that he lived in an age in which men still saw visions. It was a psychological habit, the trick of which we have forgotten ... We have nothing but dreams and we have forgotten that seeing visions – a practice now relegated to the aberrant and uneducated – was once a more significant, interesting and disciplined kind of dreaming.'[24] It is not clear which painters Eliot had in mind, but these texts point towards a secular reclamation of that habit:

> Then, pleasant to the hearing and the sight,
> The spirit joined to its beginning things
> I understood not, so profound it spake.[25]

With his rejection of the dream as 'abstracted and obscure', Mallarmé interpreted Impressionism as making material vision in several ways; expanding perception, establishing a novel way of seeing and indicating the complexity of the Subject–world relationship.

At what point may a visual image properly be said to be visionary? The question becomes important because 'Impressionism' and 'Symbolism' are interpreted as if the difference between the visual and the visionary were absolute. Mallarmé, however, reformulates the question of what is meant by 'visionary'. The word is now half-pejorative in connotation in both French and English (see note 1). The O.E.D. definitions are sceptical, and although the first of them is epistemological, it is passive, as are many definitions of Impressionism: 'capable of receiving impressions or obtaining knowledge, by means of visions'. Littré's examples nearly all imply a detachment from reality in a negative sense: 'Qui a des idées folles, extravagantes, chimériques'. Or O.E.D. again: 'fanciful', 'unreal', 'speculative', 'not actual or real', 'spectral'; that is to say, 'connoting lack of substance'. 'Speculation' most commonly connotes conjecture or unsound thinking, 'spectral', trivial ghostly imaginings.

'A mental concept of a distinct or vivid kind' may be described as a vision as well as what is perceived by the physical eye. There is no clear etymological demarcation between the mental and the physical. There is a further blurring of the distinctions between these aspects of sentience and knowledge and the 'spiritual'. A vision is 'an appearance of a prophetic or mystical character'.

Mystical, however, connotes the hidden, the enigmatic, the symbolic (in the most general sense of religious allegory) – in short the unseen. A visionary art combines powerful visualisation with revelation of the unseen, according to English roots common to the French. So the mystical is subsumed into the visionary and made clear. It is demystified and secularised, but, in these works, not de-mythified or robbed of the 'mystère' that Mallarmé strove to redefine, an emotive and generative axis to language, from language to perception and back, the freedom to play his 'jeu suprême', the language game. It is not exclusively a word game, nor does it cut entirely loose from that past which every use of language brings with it. Rather it promises, at great risk, at least the possibility of controlling these things at each language-event. This language demands and makes possible the shift in epistemology that makes visible the coherence of his arguments in 'Crise de Vers' and 'The Impressionists and Edouard Manet' as they apply to the art and literature of the nineteenth century overall. An Impressionist is a visionary; so is a Symbolist, and a Post-Impressionist and a Cubist, etc. So, potentially, is every literate:

'La différence, d'un ouvrage à l'autre, offrant autant de leçons proposées dans un immense concours pour le texte véridique, entre les âges dits civilisés ou – lettrés.' (367)

This language may be seen in operation in 'Crise de Vers' with its multiplicity of visual modes, and it relates at differing levels – of vocabulary, of argument, of metaphor and metonym – to both these separated post-Romantic currents. It not only tells us that there is a way of experiencing the work of a Redon and a Manet as coherent; it shows it.

The following quotation hinges on the appearance of words on the page and it comes in the middle of a paragraph which seeks to loosen poetic language from the Romantic author's hold and from a unitary relation to material reality and to define a 'spiritual' space in which that freedom might be structured. It combines visual signification with verbal in that it has a spatial structure in tension with the temporal. It is, furthermore, an excellent description and example of simultaneous synthesis in language:

Tout devient suspens, disposition fragmentaire avec alternance et vis-à-vis, concourant au rythme total, lequel serait le poème tu, au blancs; seulement traduit, en une manière, par chaque pendentif.

(367)

One element of the complex sentence which is the antecedent to 'tout' is visual in the common sense. It is what a page looks like. The shift of Mallarmé's text, however, is towards promoting this appearance to the levels of both syntax and semantics. It is important that this movement begins with a material surface and the action of light – important both to the metaphoric power of the text and to the weight of information it bears. This level of meaning is a vital element of why 'Un Coup de Dés' looks the way it does, and the spatial or depth component always retains this literal dimension, the spaces between words in the action of reading. But we are made to wait until the end of the sentence for the structuring figure – the 'suspens' operates until then. Scattered oppositions are proposed, maintained and then their relation is demonstrated as a dynamic structural transposition. 'Pendentif', in its primary sense here, is an architectural term for an intersection, which is the initiator of Mallarmé's meanings: 'Triangle sphérique entre les grands arcs qui supportent une coupole' (Petit Robert). The opposition of the arches and the independence of the dome are reiterated in different forms and contexts again and again in Mallarmé's writing. These interactions contribute to the connoted meaning of the passage, as does the 'disposition fragmentaire' internally. They inscribe hesitation between the oppositions. The dome is not a sufficient image. The sentence does not resolve itself into the dome and remain complete, although that shape is necessary to the apprehension of figure and meaning. The movement, from the scatter to emergent structure, remains as a residual, destablising trace.

The 'pendentif' is part of the substructure of a dome and you can see it from inside. The word in French also implies its reverse form, a jewelled pendent, a hanging faceted solid. The 'suspens' is spatial as well as temporal, and equipoise. Figure–ground reversals of this type and the notion of equipoise itself are also recurrent in Mallarmé. They are like the oppositional tension which is a structural support that underpins the dome – another opposition in turn:

Tu remarquas, on n'écrit pas, lumineusement, sur champ obscur, l'alphabet des astres, seul, ainsi s'indique, ébauché ou interrompu; l'homme poursuit noir sur blanc.   (370)

The texts propose the most extraordinary imploding and exploding space. Language as, and language at, a critical juncture – between the subject and its obliteration ('la disparition élocutoire du poète' (366), 'the painter who seems to lose his personality in Nature herself, or in the *gaze* of the multitude' (78)); between the internal and the external (. . . 'je ne sais quel miroitement, en dessous, peu séparable de la surface concédée à la rétine' (382)); between perception and conception ('prestiges situés à ce point de l'ouïe et presque de la vision abstraite, devenu l'entendement' (649)). The white and the silence – 'le poème tu, aux blancs' – again recurrent throughout Mallarmé's texts do not provide an arbitrary paradox. Nor are they always empty. They signal the unseen, the 'mystic' part of the 'vision'. In terms of signifying practice – and it is a *practice* that I am describing – they are all the subliminally perceived reflexions, crossing the signifying dichotomy between the visual and the aural sign; they are at the limits of verbal meaning and the vanishing points of comprehension.

Mallarmé's image is in some ways more flexible as a model of the transfer between conscious and unconscious mental functioning than Freud's 'mystic writing pad'.[26] Its reversals, concave to convex, mimic the relation between the optic nerve and the retina, and project the beam of light as well as receive it: 'Indépendamment de la suite ordinaire, projetés en parois de grotte' (386).

I mentioned that the movement from the scatter to the structure in the 'pendentif' image remained, leaving traces which do not allow the image to stabilise or become static. Duchamp's *Nude descending a Staircase*, for example, incorporates motion and time in this way, though the movement need not be forward or linear. In the Mallarmé text, the metaphor of the dome structures the spaces by introducing a relation of similarity between the elements of serial motion of the syntax. The metaphor is the underlying trope of lyric poetry, and the similarity-relation the major trope of 'Symbolist' art, as in Moreau. Its opposite, the metonymic relation, is one of contiguity, and this is, generally speaking, the major trope in 'realist' art, the epic or the narrative. It predominates in the Impressionism of the 1870s and 1880s which traditional art history takes as its definitive moment. The work which holds the two in relation is abstract and tends to vacillate or transmute; this is the translation to which Mallarmé refers as the action of the 'pendentif', and it is itself a good example, in language, of an abstract image.

We may amplify this by reading the paragraph before the 'pendentif' one. Mallarmé's vocabulary is that of light and is easily comprehensible in terms of the Impressionist 'mental operation' which Mallarmé discerned in *plein-air* painting as exemplified by *Le Linge* (fig. 3) and *Le Repos* (fig. 73), endowed with 'an enchanted life . . . neither personal nor sentient', in 'perpetual metamorphosis', a 'struggle ever-continued between surface and space' (75). Equally so in Cézanne's sense of the potential in appearances, of the emergent organism, which is always about to become. The tension between the lyrical and subjective (in the Romantic sense) and the attempt to define the new structures as an objectivity continuous with the components of art – sender, receiver, message and internal dynamic:

L'œuvre pure implique la disparition élocutoire de poète, qui cède l'initiative aux mots, par le heurt de leur inegalité mobilisés; ils s'allument de reflets réciproques comme une virtuelle trainée de feux sur des pierreries, remplaçant la respiration perceptible en l'ancien souffle lyrique ou la direction personnelle enthousiaste de la phrase.   (366)

The impulsion of the text is clearly ex-centric, moving between surfaces. It is a practice, not a theory; the writer and the painter do not begin with something to express, nor do they seek to impose form on chaos, nor do they merely receive impressions. They take up position. This is, necessarily, transcribed thought. It is written language, and the presence of the page is real, and active, as is the canvas as flat surface: 'Ton acte toujours s'applique à du papier; car méditer, sans traces, devient évanescent' (369).

The movement of texts of this nature is predicated on the real as a totality. Their abstraction is not a conceptualisation of the relations but a moment in their constant and energetic change. So if they imitate anything it is the illusory pause which exists only because it is thought. It relates thought and the rest of the continuum of experience. The perceived moment is deflected and becomes part of an equilibrium, internal and external, caught in passage. In formal terms this gives rise to the diffusion in Impressionism, the peculiar stasis in Seurat's Post-Impressionism and the multiplied viewpoints of Cubism. Mallarmé's *Préface* to Berthe Morisot's exhibition is a superlative example in prose-poetry of a functional transmutation of the paintings, a 'suspens de perpétuité chatoyante', a 'spectacle d'enchantement moderne':

Poétiser, par art plastique, moyen de prestiges directs, semble, sans intervention, le fait de l'ambiance éveillant aux surfaces leur lumineux secret; ou la riche analyse, chastement pour la restaurer, de la vie, selon une alchimie, – mobilité et illusion. Nul éclairage, intrus, de rêves; mais supprimés, par contre, les aspects commun ou professionel.   (536)

In formal terms, the following paragraph, isolated in the original text by large gaps, shows how Morisot's paintings work by repeating their effect in language, thus transmuting the tension between the Imaginary, the perceived and the representation.

Féerie, oui, quotidienne – sans distance, par l'inspiration, plus que le plein air enflant un glissement, le matin ou après-midi, de cygnes à nous; ni au-delà que ne s'acclimate, des ailes détournée et de tous paradis, l'enthousiaste innéité de la jeunesse dans une profondeur de journée.   (537)

'L'inspiration' here (as opposed to the 'respiration' in the paragraph quoted above beginning 'L'œuvre pure . . . ') draws in the air, but in an expansive movement. 'Inspiration' is like the passage in 'L'Après-Midi d'un Faune' where the same word occurs

> Le visible et serein souffle artificiel
> De l'inspiration, qui regagne le ciel.

The effect is 'spectral'; the ordinary scene does not disappear, but rather changes according to the action of light on the eye. At least two senses of 'spectral' are

39   Manet, *Portrait of Berthe Morisot*

40   Morisot, *Jeune Fille cueillant des Oranges*, 1889

relevant: first, the Epicurean sense of an image supposed to emanate from the corporeal or some phenomenon of reflection, and second the more analytic sense of diffraction, the breakdown of the beam of light to make visible the appearance observable in the spectrum.[27]

On the level of image-making, then, the question of representational imagery is neither primary nor simple. How do we read it as relating to the abstract, the fantastic, or dream; how literal is it, what do we mean by literal? Is literal according to the word?

Valéry aligned Mallarmé's 'pure' poetry together with Impressionism in the following way. Stressing the identity of principle in seeking the expressive source of vision and language, and the importance of their historical conjunction, Valéry describes their 'sorte de mystique':

L'Impressionisme introduit une vie speculative de la vision; un impressioniste est un contemplatif dont le méditation est rétinienne: il sent son œil créer, et en relève la sensation à la hauteur d'une révélation.[28]

These terms also apply to the apparently more clearly 'visionary' 'symbolist' texts. Redon's lithograph *Il y eût peut-être une vision première essayée dans la fleur* (fig. 43) may be read as the minute concentration of the processes described above into an image of the eye. Like the 'pendentif' image in the Mallarmé passage with which I began this discussion of vision and the visionary, it has a figurative dimension: it is a metaphor of perception. It is equally unstable and multiple, and its poise between visual and aural signification explicit. As we have seen, the verbal–visual relation may be thought of as a conjunction, a compound and transmutative sign. Redon's lithograph is part of a series called *Les Origines*, each plate of which has captions. So it has a complex of verbal and visual signifiers through which its meanings may be generated. Its title is an open-ended statement of possibility, introducing the idea of a flower and of vision as standing in some initial unspecified relation based on similarity. It suggests a continuity between animal and vegetable life, and encourages speculation on the creative possibilities of unthought-of conjunctions. There is also the clearly aural mode of reading required both by the serial form inherent in Redon and by the immensely rich precipitation of metonymic chains along different axes.

Within the series *Les Origines*, for example, the third image (fig. 44) reinforces one of the suggested readings in the second (fig. 43) and also allows of a variety of possible relationships between the two. *Le polype difforme flottait sur les rivages, sorte de Cyclope souriant et hideux* bears a clear representational similarity to the flower-eye and tends to confirm the suggestion of a head in the background shading. If the image is read as a flower, according to the caption, this darker area recedes behind the lightest of the concentric circles and reverses the question-mark shapes which direct the movement of the spectator/reader's eye. The fine lines appear as rays of light. But if the shaded area is read as a head, the figure–ground relation changes so that the eye and the dark hair appear on the same plane in relation to the picture surface, as in the

41　Redon, cover design for *Les Origines*, 1883

42　Les Origines, plate 1, *Quand s'éveillait la vie au fond de la matière obscure*

43　Les Origines, plate 2, *Il y eût peut-être une vision première essayée dans la fleur*

44　Les Origines, plate 3, *Le polype difforme flottait sur les rivages, sorte de Cyclope souriant et hideux*

45　Les Origines, plate 4, *La Sirène sortait des flots vêtue de dards*

46   Les Origines, plate 5, *Le Satyre au cynique sourire*

48   Les Origines, plate 7, *L'aile impuissante n'élèvera point la bête en ces noirs espaces*

47   Les Origines, plate 6, *Il y eût des luttes et de vaines victoires*

49   Redon, *Et l'homme parut, interrogeant le sol d'où il sort et qui l'attire, il se fraya la voie vers de sombres clartés*

Cyclops image that follows it. It is a comparable hesitation between oppositions to those found in Mallarmé and on the experiential level induces uncertainty and anxiety.

'Le sens du mystère', according to Redon 'c'est d'être toujours dans l'équivoque, dans les doubles, triples aspects (images dans images) formes qui vont être ou qui le seront selon le'état d'esprit du regardeur'.[29] As in the Mallarmé, the spectator is not allowed to settle for any reading over the rest, but compelled to accept the transitions as a part of the signifying process. Similarly in Impressionist texts, the spectator is required to move between viewpoints. The fullest power of a Monet, for example, is experienced when the spectator resists the impulse towards secondary revision and retains an unfocused impression of the colour interaction between the surfaces depicted, rather than organising the spatial relationships.[30] This more equivocal way of seeing is assisted in his later large-scale and horizonless 'Nymphéas' series, for example, by the absence of any point of reference defining either the space or a viewpoint. Mallarmé described the same device and its perceptual function in Manet's *En Bateau* (fig. 11) as contributing to the mirage-effect of isolating the transient temporal as well as spatial novelty.

The similarity of the eyes referred to above, in the second and third plates in the series *Les Origines*, which nevertheless projects forward to successivity as a structuring principle, is one of several such movements within the series. Thus in the second of these plates *Il y eût peut-être une vision première, essayée dans le fleur* (fig. 43), the suggestion of a leaf-like mouth made in the earlier one is confirmed. Its grimace reappears in the fifth of the series, *Le Satyre au cynique sourire* (fig. 46). The comparison is not primarily one of shape here, but lies rather in a shift of focus from the eye to the mouth. In the polyp the dynamic axis is the tension between the eye and the black shadows below it which may be read as signifying emergent two-eyed vision, so that multiple viewpoints are suggested as one possible meaning. In the satyr, the axis is around the mouth which is, again according to the assumed incipience of the human form confirmed in the final place, *Et l'homme parut . . .* (fig. 49) at variance with the plane of the eye and the rest of the head. With the knowledge of Cubism, we can see that such a dual perspective is compatible with the representational image. The distortion may be read as indicating temporal structure, two views of the same head – the second after it has moved – and our knowledge of the head being a composite of such movements, or the memory of them. On the semantic level, this structure implies the continued presence of the earlier forms in the later, the satyr and the androgynous or bisexual sea creatures in the human.[31]

Anterior forms subsist in the memory as peripheral vision informs sight. In *Les Origines*, the exploratory and historical inquiry is conducted through multiple devices and vocabularies. When the series was first published, it was taken to be Darwinian,[32] which Redon denied, claiming that his work was not concerned with scientific knowledge.[33] Not that evolutionary theory is either simple or even exclusive to Darwin, nor that any inquiry into 'origins' implies an unidirectional progression from a fixed point, or regression to such a hypothetical point: Redon could perhaps have made a legitimate 'scientific' claim for his work.

Redon equally repudiated interpretations such as that of Huysmans in his influential chapter on Redon, entitled 'Le Monstre',[34] which ascribes a fascination with the abnormal and the horrific to Redon's image-making. The emotive tone both of the albums and of Redon's commentaries is neutral and serious, and directed to an analysis of the phenomenal world, as perceived and as thought, one which would neither limit nor distort. His best known remark, that his aim was to place 'la logique du visible au service de l'invisible',[35] stresses the need to make visible, both in the cognitive and the perceptual sense. His method of composition was to draw something like a pebble or a leaf in great detail, after which the 'need to create' would arise. Concentration on natural form thus acted to initiate his vision of invisible forms and structures, making their beauty visible: ' . . . tout ce qui est sincèrement et docilement nouveau – comme le beau d'ailleurs – porte sa signification en soi-même.'[36]

The origin towards which these images move is their own both in an immediate and in a projected sense. They are a texture of minimal elements, subject and percept, the last two culturally defined because they are always shown in flux. Their figurative vocabulary is often derivative, and composed of juxtaposed fragments. Their meaning at this point is also minimal:

'Les abrupts, hauts jeux d'aile, se mireront, aussi: qui les mène, perçoit une extraordinaire appropriation de la structure, limpide, aux primitives foudres de la logique. . . . [The artist] récuse l'injure d'obscurité – pourquoi pas, parmi le fonds commun, d'autres d'incohérence, de rabâchage, de plagiat . . .'   (386)

It is thus necessary to come to terms with the unintelligible in the construction of sense out of signs, the unintelligible in Kristeva's definition, which ' . . . n'est pas une quelconque donnée ou expérience inarticulée mais l'œuvre d'art la plus débordante de subtiles et imperceptibles constructions'.[37] The 'primitive' in these texts is their communication of inexplicable clarity beyond what they can articulate *as a vital drive towards articulation*. As Mallarmé said of Redon's Mage, the possibility of truth justifies the search for it; Mallarmé said his sympathy went directly to the Mage (fig. 53) because he was an: 'inconsolable et obstiné chercheur d'un Mystère qu'il sait ne pas exister, et qu'il poursuivra, à jamais pour cela, du deuil de son lucide désespoir, car c'eût été la Vérité!'[38]

One substantial source of difficulty lies, as I have indicated, in the fact that the languages of myth, timelessness, 'Mystère', which predominate in the late nineteenth century occlude the historical transformations which they aim to interrogate. Part of the problem as I have so far presented it derives from the fact that the polyvalence of certain texts operates on the level of representation as well as of code, and that sometimes they still 'symbolise', whereas at other times they present. This much was clearly a pertinent question to Gauguin, for example, legible in the development of his paintings and explicit in his letters about Puvis de Chavannes and Mallarmé.[39] But other texts are not eclectic in this way and they clearly move towards the iconic. Where the text is dual, both deconstructive and iconic, what was unintelligible in the old sign-system becomes part of the definition of the new system. In Mallarmé this is foregrounded in some poems. One such is 'Ses purs ongles':

> Ses purs ongles très haut dédiant leur onyx,
> L'Angoisse, ce minuit, soutient, lampadophore,
> Maint rêve vespéral brûlé par le Phénix
> Que ne recueille pas de cinéraire amphore
>
> Sur les crédences, au salon vide: nul ptyx,
> Aboli bibelot d'inanité sonore,
> (Car le Maître est allé puiser des pleurs au Styx
> Avec ce seul objet dont le Néant s'honore).
>
> Mais proche la croisée au nord vacante, un or
> Agonise selon peut-être le décor
> Des licornes ruant du feu contre une nixe,
>
> Elle, défunte nue en le miroir, encor
> Que, dans l'oubli fermé par le cadre, se fixe
> De scintillations sitôt le septuor.   (69)

The poem is its own subject. Mallarmé wrote: 'J'ai pris ce sujet d'un sonnet nul et se réfléchissant de toutes les façons . . . ' The sonnet was taken from a projected study of 'La Parole':

il est inverse, je veux dire que le sens, s'il en a un (mais je me consolerais du contraire grace à la dose de poésie qu'il renferme, ce me semble), est évoqué par un mirage interne des mots mêmes. En se laissant aller à le murmurer plusieurs fois, on éprouve une sensation assez cabalistique.[40]

This letter concerns the earlier version of the poem. Among the various changes Mallarmé later made, one involves the inscription of the 'sensation assez cabalistique' into the second line as 'L'Angoisse'. A feeling of strangeness, often accompanied by anguish, is a feature of works which are poised in this way between signifying systems, since they also fall between the systems of perception and levels of consciousness. Transformations between the vocabulary of the supernatural or of religious experience, their associated rituals, and their secularisation on the one hand, and the vocabulary of power on the other, are among some of the most startling in Mallarmé's later prose. In *Magie*, for example, aesthetics, the extinguished philosopher's stone and political economy are all mooted in considering the power of literature. The relationship between mystery and power as a historical process is a very large part of Mallarmé's investigations into, and interrogation of, aesthetic form and 'la recherche mentale', researches aiming to locate in material reality areas of experience hitherto designated as mystical.

Sound is clearly a conspicuous formal feature of this poem and I shall look at it in some detail because it illustrates further the functional similarity between Mallarmé's theory and practice, and Impressionism. The alternating rhyme remains insistent and prominent throughout successive readings, partly because 'ix' and 'or', 'yx' and 'ore' are so unusual as rhymes, and partly because opposition (of sound, of light and dark, of internal and external) is the clearest part of the poem's message. The rhyme may be read as a tonal opposition of light and dark after the pattern ironically described in 'Crise de Vers', where it is proposed as an example of the restitutive function of poetic language: 'Le souhait d'un terme de splendeur brillant, ou qu'il s'éteigne, inverse' (364). In this complex passage Mallarmé shifts between the visual and the aural at the level of the senses – 'mon sens regrette que le discours défaille à exprimer les objets par des touches y répondant en coloris ou en allure' (364) and the applicabĭlity of his words to Impressionism is clear. 'Sens' in this sentence is one of those overcharged and exact nouns, characteristic of Mallarmé. It signifies the faculty of registering the impressions of material objects, intuitive knowledge, judgement, meaning, object of thought, and direction. It is of course the case that it appears overwrought, and the presence both of irony and of the vocabulary of the occult ('Arcane étrange') are a necessary part of what Mallarmé is saying about verse as the 'complément superieur' to language. But this paranomasic connection, or 'semantic confrontation of phonemically similar words irrespective of any etymological connection',[41] is both a means of generating meaning and an indication of that aspect of language which transgresses the border-line between the aural and the visual sign, and thus establishes 'the autonomous iconic value of phonemic oppositions'. This value asserts nothing but itself.

I shall take the semantic confrontation first. In the sonnet, the word 'ptyx' was selected as a completely empty signifier, a word which had no meaning in any language at all, as we know from the letter referred to above. But as soon as it appears in a linguistic context this arrangment of letters, a linguistic vacuum, demands to be filled. Or to put it another way, 'as soon as a sound-sequence has been interpreted as a signans, it demands a signatum'.[42] In this respect the word is negatively defined, according to the patterning of the sonnet, and we know what it should not signify; it should not signify the same as any other word. It has a signified, therefore, and this is zero. Moreover that is the same as the signifier. It is a case of identity between signifier and signified. It is a word-sign, signifying a beyond to language, the possibility of word-concept, an extra-linguistic and extra-sensory event.[43]

The negative is doubled in the poem 'nul ptyx' – 'no ptyx' and 'null ptyx', proposition and negation simultaneously. The punctuation – a clear cæsura marked by a colon and the parenthesis enclosing the last two lines of the second stanza – isolate the word and the wonderful line that follows it in their sound-pocket: 'nul ptyx, / Aboli bibelot d'inanité sonore'. The almost anagrammatical 'Aboli bibelot' mimics the tonal oppositions of the poem's rhyme scheme. 'Sonore' is a homophonic rhyme with 's'honore'; 'dont le Néant s'honore', affirmation and denial. The physical presences in the poem are cancelled: the Maître is mentioned parenthetically, he is not in the empty chamber, he is at the edge of the underworld, and his drawing tears into a hollow vessel makes the reference to the river Styx resonate with the memory of Achilles' heel rather than the river's capacity to render invulnerable; mention of the Styx recalls the spot which eluded it.

This emptying can occur with a signifier, as when a word is repressed through fear. (Or indeed in a simple memory lapse, as when we say 'it's on the tip of my tongue'.) In this case we can recall its stresses or some of its letters. In the pathological case, the lexical and syntactic contexts of the signifier may remain, and it will be understood when heard. Reception is unaffected.[44] Sound-shape and rhythm are persistent semantic features.

> . . . encor
> Que, dans l'oubli fermé par le cadre, se fixe
> De scintillations sitôt le septuor.

Interestingly the final version of 'fermé' in the penultimate line may have been 'formé'. In either case the lines are their sound-shape (linguistic fact) and they concern a pattern of perceptual and mnemonic facts – 'une nixe' is projected into the frame by a series of literal mirror images to rest as a forgotten after-image.

The spatial figure of the constellation – 'le septuor' – is both a pattern and a summary, figure and ground. It comprises pulsations of light and dark which, however, by defining each other indicate mutual limits. The constellation, in this case the Great Bear, is a number of points of lights, sometimes visible, stars which are only seen at night but whose presence is known about during the day through memory; it is also a conventional sign to which mythological histories are more or less arbitrarily assigned: meaning is written into the shape. In other words, the same sign functions according to different codes, dislocating and relativising them all – a cacophony of the spheres. No signifying system is prioritised – not even the conventional – with the result that this experiment with zero signification, far from being a perverse flirtation with meaningless sound, is a return to the basis of verbal signification and an extension of cognitive potential. As with Lacan's image of batik,[45] in which he compares unconscious memory with the pattern formed by gaps left where the dye has not taken, Mallarmé's sound-shapes are a negative limit of potential.

I commented above on the line 'Aboli bibelot d'inanité sonore'. The earlier version was 'Insolite vaisseau d'inanité sonore', which is more explicit in its reaching towards the unknown ('insolite'), but crucially less precise in its phonic enactment of withdrawal from language and re-entry into it. The reversal /bo/ /li/ and /bi/ /lo/, shortened forms of the /i/ (ee) (or) of the rest of the sonnet, supported by /i/ /a/ /o/ /ore/, put into powerful practice the 'nuit-jour' sound opposition discussed by Mallarmé in the well-known passage in 'Crise de Vers' on the fundamentals of sound and meaning, whereby poetry might approach what he called supreme language, or, in semiotic terminology, perfect signification. 'Insolite vaisseau' is condensed into 'bibelot', which is more exact – a decorative object found in an interior rather than a general container – and connotes the unusual, rendering 'insolite' tautologous, and reinforcing the strangeness of the plural 'les crédences' in the preceding line – a display board, a liturgical side-altar, a tasting table. Ritual is translated in highly artificial metrical structures: 'Arcane étrange; et d'intention pas moindre, a jailli la métrique aux temps incubatoires.' (364).

'Bibelot', like a child's plaything, perhaps trivial, perhaps significant; the uncertainty is not resolved or removable at any level. From the contours of intonation to the beginning of systematic meaning, the poem's energy is kinetic. There are identifiable characteristics which demand that the poem be read in two cognitive modes, one of them asyntactic. The resultant tension creates anxiety because the reassertion of a 'beyond' to language, a word-concept, threatens to take away former clarities as it promises future sense. 'Angoisse' in the second line of 'Ses purs ongles' may be read as in apposition to the whole of the first line and to 'ce minuit'. Midnight is the moment between the end of one day and the beginning of the next, a ritual hour, and in the rest of the stanza destruction is denied. The appearance of 'L'Angoisse' is real, and yet neutral. Obliteration is a necessary defence, as the readjustment is like a re-enactment of entry into language, hearing the child's babble, which is either meaningless or on the threshold of new meaning, accompanied by a sudden inrush of comprehension and sensation telescoping experience. Meaning is pre-conscious or 'automatic' in Freud's sense of lacking what he calls the 'cathexis of attention' linked to conscious processes.[46] While the reader's consciousness may apprehend a blank, for example, when 'ptyx' is read, meanings are being generated, and when they break through in simultaneous synthesis, the sudden excess of meaning may delight or overwhelm.

'Hommage' ('à Puvis de Chavannes') may also be read in terms of this process, both in its language and in its commentary on Puvis as a painter:

> Toute Aurore même gourde
> À crisper un poing obscur
> Contre des clairons d'azur
> Embouchés par cette sourde
>
> À le pâtre avec la gourde
> Jointe au bâton frappant dur
> Le long de son pas futur
> Tant que la source ample sourde
>
> Par avance ainsi tu vis
> O solitaire Puvis
> De Chavannes
>   jamais seul
>
> De conduire le temps boire
> À la nymphe sans linceul
> Que lui découvre ta Gloire.   (72)

The meanings of 'gourde' and 'sourde' alternate, and as they also rhyme twice with each other they become mutually defining. In the first line, 'gourde' is used

50   Puvis de Chavannes, *L'Espérance*, c. 1871

adjectivally (to qualify 'Aurore') and in the fifth it is a noun. 'Sourde' is first an adjectival noun, then a verb. As adjectives, 'gourd' and 'sourd' are overlapping in meaning, indicating dullness. A gourd and a spring, however, are both sources of nourishment; in its second use here, 'sourde' means 'gushing forth'. On the one hand, constriction and emptiness, and on the other, release and plenitude. Between them is the present limbo of transition. 'Aurore' and 'cette sourde' may on one level signify the same, the former is an active construction, as subject of 'À' at the beginning of line 5, and the latter in a passive construction, 'embouchés par cette sourde'. By occurring before the main verb, this second signifier opens out the syntactic relationships like the lexical patterning. Movements and meanings oscillate. The syntax is arrested and projected forward by the sound patterns as they propose their structure within the spaces allowed by the tempered syntax and sonnet form. Semantic inversions rebound. Morphological difference may be combined with phonemic identity, for example, as with the different signification of the 'e' at the end of 'sourde' and 'gourde'. Such uncompromising repetitions and spare initial meanings promote the activity of otherwise peripheral modes or secondary structures, such as sound-shape and repeated shape-abstracts in the signified – the curve of the gourd or the horn or the jet of the stream gushing. The visual becomes important in making meaning not only in these ways but also at the basic level of stanzaic arrangement.

By extending meanings in this way, 'Hommage' and 'Ses purs ongles' refocus in time and space the relationships between consciousness, sense impressions and memory as they defy the controls of reason and strict syntax. Freud's description of the mechanism for replacing repression as part of the process of thinking becomes conscious is a useful way of looking at how Mallarmé and Impressionism work at this level of expanded meaning. In his account, the sense organs are heightened, and so is the consciousness attached to them. Impressions are met half way and memory, part of our system of notation, replaces repression. Motor discharge is converted from inward innervations to action. (This may be compared with the innervations of inner speech, silent reading and the physical way it is possible to recall a forgotten sound-shape with the tongue.) In the following quotation, Freud suggests a relation between language and the shift from unconscious to conscious perception:

It is probable that thinking was originally unconscious . . . and was directed to the relations between impressions of objects, and that it did not acquire further qualities, perceptible to consciousness, until it became connected with verbal residues.[47]

In Mallarmé the priority of the word is not so unequivocal as this, but otherwise, Freud's is an account of cognitive process that relates equally to Impressionism as to the visual and sound aspects of Mallarmé's poetry under discussion. The heightening of consciousness involves several areas of sense-making activity, and while it might seem likely that verbal sound at this degree of intensity would be manifest in 'purely' aural signification, it leads towards the visual in its reduction of syntactic, hierarchical ordering. The effect is to distort memory because although memory may replace repression, memory is also inhibited by the lack of systematic arrangement and its alteration of perception. If indeed memory and consciousness are involved in a dynamic of this kind, then we might expect a lowering of short-term memory in relation to increases in consciousness, and also to alterations in perception: towards a less differentiated relation between subject and object and between object and object, and towards a reduction in hierarchy. This is visible in the Impressionist foregrounding of peripheral vision, and in Manet's distortions of perspective, for example in *Un Déjeuner sur l'Herbe* (fig. 8). Thinking and perceiving in this way are syncretic, involving the whole person, so that the blanks in memory may also be experienced as blanks in feeling. In 'L'Après-Midi d'un Faune' the Faune's visions and memories are punctuated indifference and gaps in his hold on sense and sensation:

> Inerte, tout brûle dans l'heure fauve
> Sans marquer par quel art ensemble détala
> Trop d'hymen souhaité de qui cherche le 'la':   (51)

The economy of 'Ses purs ongles' and 'Hommage' is a refinement of the exploration of memory, perception and consciousness in 'L'Après-Midi d'un Faune'. They follow a rhythm of tension and release in which relations are telescoped with a sudden and intense heightening of recollected sense impressions and thought. Such impressions are not organised primarily by syntax, but according to a musical 'syntax of equivalences', and may be accompanied by a sense of *déjà-vu*, since they bring to consciousness for the first time sensory and unconscious impressions. This is part of their theme, re-enacted through the successive readings they require if their full power is to be felt. The concentration of these effects is in itself a source of anxiety as a part of their emotive quality, most poignant at the point of minimal meaning where it becomes its own meaning, another example of the drive of the texts towards introversive or musical signification, the uniting of signifier and signified. At this fleeting point where the verbal and the visual function in the same way, if only for a moment, they break down the polarity of irreconcilable, but not fixed, dualisms in signification – 'not fixed' in that components may take over from each other, though they never synthesise: figure–ground reversals, verbal signs in which space is the structural principle, and visual signs in which time is the structural principle. All other oppositions may be similarly placed in variable relations generative of energy and meaning directed towards discharge of excess and repose. The tone of the last words of both 'L'Après-Midi d'un Faune' ('Couple, adieu; je vais voir l'ombre que tu devins') and 'Un Coup de Dés' ('Toute pensée émet un Coup de Dés.') is neutral. The colours in Impressionism, as in the spectrum or in Seurat's colour theory,[48] maintain their vivid separateness in their limpid surface tension. Manet's *Un Bar aux Folies Bergères* (fig. 35), like Gauguin's *D'où venons-nous, que sommes-nous, où allons-nous?*, has just such a structure in formal and in semantic terms, the colour component of which is predicated on the complementaries, blue and orange. The central figure maintains her neutral, undifferentiated expression, her reflections are male and female, the spaces are not ambiguous, they are clearly in differing relation to any given fixed point. Oscillations between meanings thus may be seen to signify a transgressive desire. From tension and intense energy to entropic release, the subject desires incorporation and to incorporate. The desire to unite signifier and signified is accompanied by the desire to unite the sender of the message, the absent 'Le Maître' of 'Ses purs ongles' or the central figures in *Un Bar aux Folies Bergères* and *D'où venous-nous, que sommes-nous, où allons-nous?*, with the other. An existential relation between the Subject and the sign-system is implied and the physical body and the language-body increasingly implicated. This is evident in the recurrent theme in Mallarmé of the physical act of writing. The desire to merge the gestural mark on the page into direct thought presentation develops from a theme into a structural principle in 'Un Coup de Dés':

Fiançailles

    dont
        le voile d'illusion rejailli leur hantise
        ainsi que le fantôme d'un geste

            chancellera
            s'affalera

            folie   (464)

The 'Maître' in the poem is shadowed by his past self both as an individual and through history ('l'ultérieur démon immémorial'); the letter and the dark mark on the page repeat the beginning of recorded sound and historical re-presentation. The magnitude of such a concentration of time is part of the poem's reversals of scale, its power and its madness.

We have already seen how sound-gesture functions in 'Ses purs ongles'. In *Les Mots Anglais* Mallarmé outlines the tension and release mechanism at the basis of intonational meaning, and therefore of all meaning since it is the part of the language system the child first learns:

(F)

Lettre d'un valeur très particulière, quoique commmençant moins de mots que 'b' et 'p', deux des autres labiales, F indique de soi une étreinte forte et fixe, c'est devant les voyelles et les dipthongs: unie aux liquides ordinaires 'b' et 'r', elle forme avec 'l' la plupart des vocables représantant l'acte de voler ou battre l'espace, même transposé par la rhétorique dans la région des phénòmenes lumineux, ainsi que l'acte de couler, comme dans les langues classiques; avec 'r' c'est tantôt la lutte ou l'éloignement, tantôt plusieurs sens point apparentés entre eux.   (p. 935)

51   Redon, *Le Masque de la Mort Rouge*, 1883

Both in this passage and in the lists of words beginning with 'f' which Mallarmé cites we can see how the transpositions in his generative system begin to assume concrete expression. Both flying and beating space under constraint, for example, are signified by the wing which modulates through peoms such as 'Le vierge le vivace' (as intricate in its sound patterns as 'Ses purs ongles') and 'Quand l'ombre menaça' and in the synecdochic[49] feather thrown up in 'Un Coup de Dés', 'plume solitaire

52   Redon, *Sous l'aile d'ombre, l'être noir*
       appliquait une active morsure,
       from the series *Songes,* 1891

éperdue' (possibly a vestigial interlingual pun, extending 'plume' in French to 'aigrette' or 'plume' in English).

   These signs enact the spatial and gestural dimension of the genesis of sound-meaning. But *Les Mots Anglais*, though written as a text book, is a historical study of language, and it is therefore about written language, the enactment of sound become trace. 'Feather', 'plume' with their two cognitive modes, heard and seen,

   Écrire –
L'encrier, cristal comme une conscience, avec sa goutte, au fond de ténèbres relative à ce que quelque chose soit: puis, écarte la lampe.   (370)

With emotion and desire at its origins 'l'omniprésent Ligne espacée de tout point à tout autre pour instituer l'idée' makes the historical, the psychic density of a thought externally visible – at least in germ – thereby altering the whole system of internal and external economies. Invariance in this sense precedes both coding and systematic organisation and therefore does not smuggle in the old eternal verities. The problem the texts address is how the new perception might insert itself into the system, for unless some systematised relation can emerge from the confrontation of new and old meaning, the new may remain incommunicable. It is very likely to be incomprehensible and to be resisted. How the texts embody this problem of adjustment may be further clarified through Freud's notion of 'ideational mimetics'. Although on one level this concept may refer merely to a tautologous gesture

53 Hommage à Goya, 1885, plate 1,
Dans mon Rêve, je vis au ciel un visage de mystère

55 Hommage à Goya, plate 3,
Un fou dans un morne paysage

54 Hommage à Goya, plate 2,
La fleur du marécage, une tête humaine et triste

56 Hommage à Goya, plate 4,
Il y eût aussi des êtres embryonnaires

accompanying thought, on another it provides a descriptive framework for the transposition of energies between levels of perception, innervation, ideation both in communication and in the internal formation of an idea. As an asyntactic or 'primitive' thought mode, within but not absorbed by linguistically governed concepts it is most fully realised in 'Un Coup de Dés', but other modes in which an existential relation between signifier and signified is either the basis or one of the

57 Hommage à Goya, plate 5, *Un étrange jongleur*

58 Hommage à Goya, plate 6, *Au réveil, j'aperçus*
la Déesse de l'Intelligible au profil sévère et dur

bases also attempt to confront old meaning with new method. Projected analogues between the mental and physical world, such as Mallarmé's chimeras in 'Igitur', whose 'suprêmes frissons' fed his narrator's terror at his reflection, emerging from the dark 'avec leurs anneaux convulsifs' or again where the furnishings seemed to 'tordre leurs chimères' perform the transfer on the level of shape. This may be compared with 'Un Coup de Dés', on the page which figures a 'tourbillon d'hilarité et d'horreur' (466–7). Less Gothic examples from painting may be found for instance in Moreau (*Œdipe et le Sphinx*, *la Chimère* – not illustrated), in Gauguin, or many others, and these texts move towards retranslation of classical mythology by formal and iconographical allusion. In this the texts are less iconic; their relation to the signified is more conventional, and their function more static in that they refer to an episode in the narrative (the myth or story) without advancing it diegetically or relaying it to some adjacent, analogical or structurally similar image or text.

These formal disjunctions, then, have varying semiotic functions, among which the combination of conventional and existential relations, after the model of the shifter, with which I began, is the most innovatory. A further, related type of semiosis is that of distortion,[50] seen in grotesque or caricatural drawing and in Mallarmé in syntactic distortions, and assisted in 'Un Coup de Dés' by the graphemic[51] activity of the varying type-faces and their distribution forming black and white patterns.

Redon's series *Hommage à Goya* (figs. 53–58) compares with 'Quand l'ombre menaça' at the level of images and so offers an accessible example. The poem also compares at the same level with the death-figures (figs. 64 and 65) and, in the verbal chain, inserts into the wing series in Mallarmé ('Il a ployé son aile indubitable en moi', stanza 1). But I shall focus on the second stanza in conjunction with *Dans mon rêve, je vis au ciel un visage de mystère'* (fig. 53) and *Un étrange jongleur* (fig. 57) respectively.

> Luxe, ô salle d'ébène où, pour séduire un roi
> Se tordent dans leur mort des guirlandes célèbres,
> Vous n'êtes qu'un orgueil menti par les ténèbres
> Aux yeux du solitaire ébloui de sa foi.

This poem is of course a regular sonnet, and, in terms of syntax, there is nothing very unusual about this stanza. Nor might it be said to be conceptually difficult, or lexically arcane. If it makes no direct impression of clear meaning, it is because its meanings are transferred between internal and external elements. Though it may signify absence of meaning, its signified is not at all simple or unitary. Part of this is due to the way its intense sensuous impact carries an abstract meaning. The king and the solitary are as attributes almost, worldly abundance and pride, or faith. Since 'luxe' is phonologically the same as 'lux', and both figures are dazzled, the ebony chamber and the illusion appear common to both the senses and the spirit. 'Solitaire', especially with its proximity to 'guirlandes', also signifies diamond or crystalline structure when taken as part of the verbal chain in Mallarmé which is based on the page itself, the constellation whose pattern makes visible the structure of writing. It appears in the last stanza of the poem as 'astre en fête'. The signified is located as the *relationship* established at the level of the signifier. This transgresses the division between matter and spirit, king and solitary, and an alteration in both is proposed. The manner of this distortion allows access to thought and perception at a greater level of dedifferentiation than rational or any more unitary (visual or aural) process, the function of caricature as controlled regression: the inhibition against playing with thought is lifted.

This is like the 'principle of assistance' described by Freud as the initial part of his 'fore-pleasure' principle in the joke-work.[52] Distinguishing between verbal and conceptual jokes, Freud extends this binary structure to the pleasure generated, a core in play and a further element in lifting inhibitions. The implication of Freud's outline is not only that the interaction between the verbal and conceptual levels allows greater generation of pleasure but also that it provides a further source of pleasure in thought and non-sense (in some combination) which would otherwise be suppressed. This can be effected, in the same movement as the fore-pleasure principle and its obstruction of pleasure leading to an increase, by assuming the pretence of meaning where there is none – an aspect of Mallarmé's 'art consacré aux fictions' (368). In both of these there is a lapse of time involved and a discrepancy between the expectations raised and the result, both in terms of pleasure and of meaning. The lapse of time, its initiating bewilderment and consequent increase of attention outline a mode such as that of simultaneous synthesis. In Freud's words,

'The nonsense that still remains in a conceptual joke acquires secondarily the function of increasing our attention by bewildering us. It serves as a means of intensifying the effect of a joke, but only when it acts obtrusively, so that the bewilderment can hurry ahead of the understanding by a perceptible moment in time.'[53] The question of attention is important in this particular combination with bewilderment and play, juxtaposing productively otherwise incompatible conceptual modes. 'Reason, critical judgement, suppression' are inimical to the fore-pleasure principle, which 'holds fast to the original sources of verbal pleasure'. But then word-play works by more indirect means than conscious processes, and is more properly described as pre-conscious or 'automatic'.[54] Abstract thought, however, displaces fewer energies than action, although in terms of movement, the physical memory of 'innervatory expenditure' alone may come to represent the idea. As with the comic of movement[55] the effect arises from an over-large expenditure of energy. The trace of these transferrals between abstract and physical levels may be seen in caricatural distortion of the body or facial features in drawing because these appear as the trace of exaggerated movement.[56] That movement, as I have described above as 'ideational mimetics', is the idea.

Not surprisingly, there is foreboding and triumph in 'Quand l'ombre menaça' and in the *Hommage à Goya*, for they intuit the unobtainable and cannot afford a return of sense for the energies displaced, at least not in themselves. Their mode of being is projected forwards. As we have seen from Mallarmé's response to the first plate of *Hommage à Goya* (fig. 53), with its enlarged eye and nose and shrunken hand he identified with it as an image not of pessimism but of infinite and insatiable desire. In 'Un Coup de Dés' too, desire goes further than the body will allow, and the psychic drives the physical beyond its limits. The body must adapt, either itself or its surroundings, or turn back on the psyche.

Thus when Redon's caricatural distortions in *Un étrange jongleur* (fig. 57) make an eye appear ready to leave the body and join the celestial spheres whose shape it echoes, they make an alteration to the possibilities both psychic and physical. They desire to see more, and in making the sign of that desire, begin to open out the space for it to enter the system. The level of regression is very deep, deeper than dreams because the wish is incarnated, not represented. At this level, the body and sign-body has only itself that it can affect to bring about the desired end, and to effect change.

4

'UN COUP DE DÉS' AS ILLUSTRATED POEM

Redon's trial illustrations for 'Un Coup de Dés'

Mallarmé and Redon met in 1885, probably through J.-K. Huysmans and became lifelong friends.[1] Mallarmé's admiration and understanding of Redon's work is clear from their correspondence.[2] In 1897–8 they worked on the illustrated edition of 'Un Coup de Dés', to be published by Vollard with four illustrations, though only three remain. Mallarmé wanted the illustrations to be dark in overall effect to offset the white of the poem, so he clearly thought of the lithographs as working in conjunction with the written text.[3] It is not clear exactly why the project was not completed, but it was in hand when Mallarmé died in 1898. The following February, Geneviève Mallarmé, the poet's daughter, invited Redon to draw a frontispiece for the posthumous edition, but he apparently did not.[4]

59–61   Redon, illustrations for 'Un Coup de Dés', 1898

UN COUP DE DÉS

JAMAIS

QUAND BIEN MÊME LANCÉ DANS DES CIRCONSTANCES
ÉTERNELLES

DU FOND D'UN NAUFRAGE

SOIT
que

l'Abîme

blanchi
étale
furieux

sous une inclinaison
plane désespérément

d'aile

la sienne

par

avance retombée d'un mal à dresser le vol
et couvrant les jaillissements
coupant au ras les bonds

très à l'intérieur résume

l'ombre enfouie dans la profondeur par cette voile alternative

jusqu'adapter
à l'envergure

sa béante profondeur en tant que la coque

d'un bâtiment

penché de l'un ou l'autre bord

LE MAÎTRE

surgi
    inférant

                de cette conflagration

                      que se

                 comme on menace

           l'unique Nombre qui ne peut pas

                      hésite
               cadavre par le bras
plutôt
     que de jouer
        en maniaque chenu
         la partie
        au nom des flots
                    un

           naufrage cela

　　　　hors d'anciens calculs
　　　　où la manœuvre avec l'âge oubliée

　　　　　　　jadis il empoignait la barre

à ses pieds
　　　　　de l'horizon unanime

prépare
　　s'agite et mêle
　　　　au poing qui l'étreindrait
un destin et les vents

être un autre

　　　　　　Esprit
　　　　　　　　pour le jeter
　　　　　　　　　　　dans la tempête
　　　　　　　　en reployer la division et passer fier

écarté du secret qu'il détient

envahit le chef
coule en barbe soumise

direct de l'homme

　　　sans nef
　　　　　n'importe
　　　　　　　　où vaine

ancestralement à n'ouvrir pas la main
crispée
par delà l'inutile tête

legs en la disparition

à quelqu'un
ambigu

l'ultérieur démon immémorial

ayant
de contrées nulles
induit
le vieillard vers cette conjonction suprême avec la probabilité

celui
son ombre puérile
caressée et polie et rendue et lavée
assouplie par la vague et soustraite
aux durs os perdus entre les ais

né
d'un ébat
la mer par l'aïeul tentant ou l'aïeul contre la mer
une chance oiseuse

Fiançailles

dont
le voile d'illusion rejailli leur hantise
ainsi que le fantôme d'un geste

chancellera
s'affalera

folie

N'ABOLIRA

COMME SI

Une insinuation

au silence

dans quelque proche

voltige

simple

enroulée avec ironie
               ou
                   le mystère
                          précipité
                               hurlé

tourbillon d'hilarité et d'horreur

autour du gouffre
                   sans le joncher
                         ni fuir

             et en berce le vierge indice

                                       COMME SI

plume solitaire éperdue

sauf

que la rencontre ou l'effleure une toque de minuit
et immobilise
au velours chiffonné par un esclaffement sombre

cette blancheur rigide

dérisoire
en opposition au ciel
trop
pour ne pas marquer
exigüment
quiconque

prince amer de l'écueil

s'en coiffe comme de l'héroïque
irrésistible mais contenu
par sa petite raison virile
en foudre

soucieux
       expiatoire et pubère

                   muet

La lucide et seigneuriale aigrette
       au front invisible
scintille
       puis ombrage
une stature mignonne ténébreuse
    en sa torsion de sirène

par d'impatientes squames ultimes

rire

que

SI

de vertige

debout

le temps
de souffleter
bifurquées

un roc

faux manoir
tout de suite
évaporé en brumes

qui imposa
une borne à l'infini

C'ÉTAIT

issu stellaire

CE SERAIT

pire

non

davantage ni moins

indifféremment mais autant

LE NOMBRE

EXISTÂT-IL
autrement qu'hallucination éparse d'agonie

COMMENÇÂT-IL ET CESSÂT-IL
sourdant que nié et clos quand apparu
enfin
par quelque profusion répandue en rareté
SE CHIFFRÂT-IL

évidence de la somme pour peu qu'une
ILLUMINÂT-IL

LE HASARD

Choit
la plume
rythmique suspens du sinistre
s'ensevelir
aux écumes originelles
naguères d'où sursauta son délire jusqu'à une cime
flétrie
par la neutralité identique du gouffre

RIEN

de la mémorable crise
ou se fût
l'événement

accompli en vue de tout résultat nul
                              humain

        N'AURA EU LIEU
      une élévation ordinaire verse l'absence

                QUE LE LIEU
inférieur clapotis quelconque comme pour disperser l'acte vide
             abruptement qui sinon
           par son mensonge
             eût fondé
            la perdition

dans ces parages
        du vague
            en quoi toute réalité se dissout

EXCEPTÉ

à l'altitude

PEUT-ÊTRE

aussi loin qu'un endroit

fusionne avec au delà

          hors l'intérêt
         quant à lui signalé
                  en général
selon telle obliquité par telle déclivité
                de feux

   vers
      ce doit être
        le Septentrion aussi Nord

UNE CONSTELLATION

       froide d'oubli et de désuétude
               pas tant
            qu'elle n'énumère
     sur quelque surface vacante et supérieure
          le heurt successif
                sidéralement
     d'un compte total en formation

veillant
   doutant
      roulant
        brillant et méditant

          avant de s'arrêter
        à quelque point dernier qui le sacre

       Toute Pensée émet un Coup de Dés

The idea of reading 'Un Coup de Dés' as an *illustrated* text is not an easy one to assimilate. Most people are surprised to discover that it was originally going to be published in this form. Illustration seems not to fit at all, as I said earlier, within the existing 'modernist' framework of reading. This has to do in part with the form of the two parts of the illustrated text. The written and the lithographic texts appear at first sight to be poles apart. I have tried to show in the preceding chapter that this is not in fact the case. It appears so because of the way the texts have since been constructed – or ignored. Furthermore we do not value illustration, or transpositions between verbal and visual signs, and still find visual material hard to integrate with serious written texts, even though we can accommodate words and images in film or in comics and advertising. This is partly because of hierarchies of form, and partly because the way we direct verbal consciousness separates it from other ways of knowing. It is also because we still prefer to read texts as discrete.

'Un Coup de Dés' may be read as an attack on these habits of thought. In reading it constructively with Redon's illustrations we have to rethink what we understand as visual expression and move outside the boundaries of the texts to experience them as open-ended. They are a book with interchangeable pages, with varying directions and registers, with vertical and horizontal movements, with reversals and with shapes that are as important in signification as words. They challenge our notion of coherence and demand that we re-shape the relations between recorded and immediate experience. Or if this seems too large a claim, we can bring to them our dissatisfaction with the ways we articulate areas of cultural experience and find that they afford an opening. This is what draws me to them as a feminist and as a writer.

Play is one of the main ways through which the poem explores the possibilities of reconstructing sense. The game entails risk, fear, uncertainty and pleasure. Although pleasure is the least explicit, it is far from being the least important of the poem's elusive ways of making and deflecting meaning. But to remove the constraints governing the use of language, so that everything is *at play*, as in 'Un Coup de Dés', the poem risks non-sense. It offers the reader no assurances as it erodes the comparative safety of rational modes. Le Maître in 'Un Coup de Dés':

hésite

cadavre par le bras   écarté du secret qu'il détient

plutôt

que de jouer

en maniaque chenu

la partie

au nom des flots   (462–3)

The emotive quality of this game is imaged in the following complete page, bounded by conditionals, symmetrical on the surface, but over-laying the appalling vortex. This detachment is not a mere attitude, but both a temporal separation and the mechanism through which resistance is overcome and the inhibition against verbal pleasure is lifted. Further, the detachment is maintained because word-play lacks the 'cathexis of attention', releasing energies whose displacement covertly distorts still further the secondary, restraining structures:

COMME SI

     Une insinuation *simple*
      au silence *enroulée avec ironie*

              ou

            le mystère

              précipité

                 hurlé

    dans quelque proche *tourbillon d'hilarité et d'horreur*
       voltige *autour du gouffre*

             sans le joncher

                ni fuir

         et en berce le vierge indice

                COMME SI
                 (466–7)

Attention is so concentrated that at the moment of satisfaction, consciousness is lost. This is inscribed into the white spaces of poem and the necessity of scanning the pages to follow the poem's movements. The text communicates while the reader performs these seemingly empty motions. Pleasure is combined with unpleasure and loss of control. In the waiting, it is not at all clear how to break through, or from where the initiative should derive. If from the poem, then from which aspect, and with what degree of active compliance with its movements?

    LE MAÎTRE   hors d'anciens calculs
         où la manoeuvre avec l'âge oubliée

            jadis il empoignait la barre (462–3)

The tensions thus set in motion are the basic condition of reading, and they form part of a process in which resistance is overcome and the return through all the poem's treacherous vortices made possible. Some of the experience of unpleasure comes from the fact that the economic problem involved in this defusing process – that is, the dissipation of energies in the effort simply to direct events and track their movements within and outside the reader, between the subject and the sign – reproduces the transposition of affects of a phase of development whose residue may be seen in masochism. This phase involves the binding of the death instinct to the libido to control the power of emergent aggressive tendencies either to attack the Subject or to direct themselves outwards. An important part of the poem's cultural message is indicated by 'Le Maître's' power struggle, as the internal dynamics of the poem reproduce, yet contain, the destructive tendencies endemic in the movement from instinctual or uncoded modes, a most powerful admixture of primary operations with successive phases. The erosion of attack, covering over earlier layers, as in the repression of the male or the female elements in the psyche to allow supremacy to one gender is allied to the 'culturing' process and unitary thinking in which part of the energies expended is directed against alternative modes. The poem derives its implosive violence from its refusal of this focusing and repressing operation.

Coupant au ras les bonds   (461)

Let us look more closely at this dynamic in both the written and the lithographic text by taking the word 'aigrette' (470). Part of the meaning of 'aigrette' is the conventional one of a crest, and this may be taken as relating to the plumed head-dress of the crysalid. This conventional relation may be read as working as the 'anchor'. In neither the poem nor the lithograph (fig. 60), as we would expect, is the sign unitary, and this multiplies the ways in which they may be read in relation to each other, or used to construct a joint signified. Still at the level of conventional relations, 'aigrette' also signifies the white crest of the wave, together with the 'stature mignonne et ténébreuse' and the whole figure of the chrysalid. There is a movement in the lexical sign towards the visual because the relay function is performed by shape. That is, the curve may be abstracted from all these elements – the plume, the chrysalid, the wave – and successively overlaid in serial motion. In this it is comparable with the 'patriarch' movement discussed above in Freud (pages 00ff.), and in both Mallarmé and Redon such transformations are a major affective function occurring at the point of transfer between thought structures and sensory perceptions. Put another way, when image and word presentation have equal weight, relationships further to the conventional are implied, often introducing a sudden sensation that the sign is unstable or out of control. For example, one such relationship reverses the relay function. Within the poem and the lithographic series, within the totality of Mallarmé's and Redon's production, signs and their elements overlap. This imbrication is not the same as association or connotation, since it is only partially a function of language on the one hand and iconography on the other. The movement in the sign is basically a structural function made possible by the 'emptying' effect seen and heard in, for example, 'Ses purs ongles' and its 'inanité sonore'. The disintegrative effect of Impressionism is comparable in this respect with Redon's ambiguities of space and light and introduces additional axes, which unnervingly seem to switch from meaning to nothingness, as the emotive charge reduces to zero and neutralises the cathected energies. So, having moved off from the initiating signifier – from the crest in the present example – whole series of signifying chains are set up and cancelled within the text. Sound, shape and meaning telescope into the initiating signifier, as in the dream-work or the hysterical mechanism of condensation. The 'aigrette' in this presentation is other than, and not reducible to, the independent word as an element in the lexicon. Like the near-homophonous lines of 'Prose pour des Esseintes', for example, the boundaries of the word are effectively altered. 'Non de visions' and nous en devisions' (stanza 6) merge: forms of representation in the poem combine apparently making

62 Redon, *L'Intelligence fût à moi!*
Je devins le Buddha

64 Redon, *C'est une tête de mort avec une couronne de roses.*
Elle domine une torse de femme d'une blancheur nacrée

63 Redon, *Et il avait dans sa main droite sept étoiles*
et de sa bouche sortait une epée aigüe à deux tranchants

65 Redon, *La Mort: mon ironie dépasse tous les autres!*

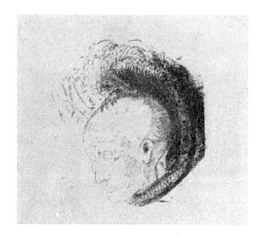

66   Redon, frontispiece for *Le Mouvement Idéaliste en
Peinture* by Mellerio, 1896

67   Redon, *Mes baisers ont le gout d'un fruit qui se fondrait
dans ton coeur . . . Tu me dédaignes! Adieu*

only minimal reference to anything apart from themselves and each other. They simply *are*. But their mode of signification is more complex: the message is received both as simple percepts and as percepts of the more unexpected kind that occur when the abstract is interrupted and expresses the actual content of the thought. In the lithograph, the chrysalid is in part a conventional Western drawing of a head – without, for example, the ambiguities of perspective or distortions visible in others of Redon's lithographs, such as *Le polype difforme flottait sur les rivages, sorte de Cyclope souriant et hideux* (fig. 44) or the Mage of *Dans mon Rêve, je vis au ciel un visage de mystère* (fig. 53). It is also an abstract of motion, a curve with the sketch lines out of which it sprang. Comparison with the Buddha *L'Intelligence fût à moi! Je devins le Buddha* (fig. 62) shows a similar emergent form, where the body appears as two crossed casings, or a coiled snake-like form, which compare with the wing-shaped casing both of the overall chrysalid and of the shoulder where it splits open.

The chrysalid also signifies abstract ideas, both within its own series and intertextually with others in Redon, setting up a relay to his death figures, spiritual affirmation and triumph over the body poised against death or instinctual gratification. Thus the chrysalid of 'Un Coup de Dés' relays not only to the image I have just mentioned, *L'Intelligence fût à moi! Je devins le Buddha* (fig. 62), but also to the saint in *Et il avait dans sa main droite sept étoiles, et de sa bouche sortait une epée aigüe à deux tranchants* (fig. 63) and at the same time and with the same signifier of shape to *C'est une tête de mort avec une couronne de roses. Elle domine une torse de femme d'une blancheur nacrée* (fig. 64), and to *La Mort: mon ironie dépasse toutes les autres!* (fig. 65). Both on the emotive and the ideational axis the chrysalid resembles the vision of 'Quand l'ombre menaça':

> Luxe, ô salle d'ébène où, pour séduire un roi
> Se tordent dans leur mort des guirlandes célèbres. (67)

Within the series of 'Un Coup de Dés' this pattern of repeated curves also extends to the sea-horse on the woman's helmet (fig. 59) which combines the emergent reptile of *Le Mouvement Idéaliste en Peinture* (fig. 66) with the helmet of the temptress from *La Tentation de Saint Antoine* (fig. 67). The reptile's head is in metamorphosis, and the woman of 'Un Coup de Dés' has a half-mask, half-dice before her face. This texture resembles 'Victorieusement fui le suicide beau', which, together with 'Quand l'ombre menaça', is one of four sonnets whose theme relates closely to this one:

> La tienne si toujours le delice! la tienne
> Oui seule qui du ciel évanoui retienne
> Un peu de puéril triomphe en t'en coiffant
>
> Avec clarté quand sur les coussins tu la poses
> Comme un casque guerrier d'impératrice enfant
> Dont pour te figurer il tomberait des roses. (68)

In the lithographs the images have a broad cultural range of reference, deriving from Flaubert, from various mythologies and from the Bible, making a rich field of connoted meaning connected with death and metamorphosis. Where there are captions to the image, these advance, but may also deflect, diegesis – the linguistic message brings in additional information from outside the image which may either direct the serial motion along the same axis as the abstract shape or across it. The images are thus multiple in form and derivation and in their transitional structures between visual and aural signs they bear an existential relation to these meanings.

Clearly the illustrated text offers new and exciting potential – what kind of reading does it require? How might it reveal the transformations between signs, Subjectivity and the way reality comes to be represented mentally and so that they may be as initiating and liberating? In what further ways is visual form an active part of the process of making meanings and understanding them as they are generated? And how do 'illustrations' fit in? To read in Mallarmé is to see things happen:

Lire–

Cette pratique–

Appuyer, selon la page, au blanc, qui l'inaugure son ingénuité, à soi, oublieuse même du titre qui parlerait trop haut: et, quand s'aligna, dans une brisure, la moindre, disseminée, le hasard vaincu mot par mot, indéfectiblement le blanc revient . . .

Virginité qui solitairement, devant une transparence du regard adéquat, elle-même s'est comme divisée en ses fragments de candeur, l'un et l'autre, preuves nuptiales de l'Idée.   (386–7)

The nature of the visual in 'Un Coup de Dés' touches the heart of the matter. It ranges from the simple poem-as-seen, with signifiers such as typography and lay-out to the complex linguistic structures outlined in chapter 3, which move thought towards the simultaneity of perception. Both these extremes counter the forward and horizontal motion of the poem and inscribe temporal reversals of the kind explored lexically in the poem. The visual form is semantic in that it supplies a minimal indication of the meanings lost in the words. In requiring the reader to take up a position in relation to its shapes as they appear to the eye, while maintaining fragments of syntax, the poem connects language with seeing and, by extension, articulate with perceived knowledge.

The poem demands a degree of self-observation while reading and requires of readers that they relate what they experience to its own reflexive processes. Rather than centering the relation of language to language, the formal innovations direct the reader outside coded reality to lived experience and the interchanges between the mind, the body and the material world, integrating the sign-body with experience.

Mallarmé's preface to the poem is about reading, but it is not a guide. Nor does it offer a theory of reading. Its tone is uncertain, I find, containing distant echoes of 'Crise de Vers' and 'La Musique et les Lettres', but with a certain diffidence about the crucial question of how far it goes beyond the framework outlined in these texts. Mallarmé allies the poem with *vers libre* and the prose-poem, both important developments, as he outlined in 'Crise de Vers', and proposes that his text should be read as a new genre, like the symphony, a genre in which literature recovers from music something of its lost resources, as he explained in *La Musique et les Lettres*. Yet there are hints that allow the reader to formulate a kind of reading that does indeed break with tradition, and these in part contradict the suggestion that the poem is 'un "état" qui ne rompe pas de tout point avec la tradition' (456). One such clue is the apparent disclaimer, 'le tout sans nouveauté qu'un espacement de lecture' (455). This spacing out of the process of reading does not leave tradition untouched, nor does the concomitant alteration of pace, introducing several perspectives and temporal movements at the same point in the text. Mallarmé's descriptions of the breaks, returns and re-formations of text as it accelerates and slows down stress their identity with mental process and yet also treat the text as autonomous. Thus, for example, he writes of 'cet emploi à nu de la pensée avec retraits, prolongements, fuites' and of the separate movements of the text: 'Le papier intervient chaque fois qu'une image, d'elle-même, cesse ou rentre'; 'La fiction affleurera et se dissipera, vite, d'après la mobilité de l'écrit' (455). Textual and mental space transgress each other. Furthermore the spatial and temporal elements are semantic. This has implications both for reading the text as an entity and for reading it as open-ended, as a composite text which generates its meanings internally and with other texts. This allows space for reading it with the lithographs Redon made for it, not just as an illustrated poem but with the lithographs as an extension of the visual element of the text itself.

There are at least three ways in which this incorporation and extension can be brought about. First, since the kind of reading demanded is discontinuous, one in which attention is transferred from strictly syntactic operations to the visual appearance of the page, it requires no interference with the reading process to read the lithographs. This is not true of the traditional written text. Second, the visual meanings from within the language, such as simultaneous synthesis and the other formal structures discussed in the preceding chapter, initiate the move towards visual thought-patterns. Finally the lithographs themselves operate a similar variation in levels and semantic mode, containing differing registers of visual expression and moving towards verbal structures. Reading their formal meaning is therefore an exercise compatible with that of reading the written text.

The effect of these innovations on the practice of reading may be clearer if we take account of Barthes's observations on reading, addressed to Lucette Finas: 'Le classicisme (au sens très large du terme), dont nous vivons encore, a établi une norme du débit de lecture, un rhythme optimal que l'on doit imprimer à l'œil–intelligence qui lit, en deça ou au-delà duquel il n'y a que démence et non-sens.'[5] Barthes goes on to refer to Pascal's law of reading and of looking at paintings, both subject to a classical, unified perspective in which only one point is the right one from which to view and one rhythm the right one for reading. Finas, he says, intervenes in the text to ruin these norms, and in so doing effects for the text the same development as has been happening in painting since the beginning of the century. This may or may not be the case as regards Finas herself. It is certainly true that multiple perspectives have not been recognised in the text in the same way as in painting, though it is implicit in the recent intervention of women's writing, with its demand for new rhythms of reading and new meanings.

In establishing what Barthes calls 'tempo' as semantic ('un élément constituant du sens'), reading itself becomes a text which refuses to be recuperated by 'Une construction de l'homme'.[6] Reading 'Un Coup de Dés' similarly defies recuperation both in tempo and in spatial terms. This is especially true of the dual lithographic and written text. This is not necessarily to say that it did so in 1898. It does now; since it is an open text-in-process, since reading generates the text. It does not need to be 'placed' historically at one moment. What it signified when it was written can only be reconstructed, and has importance only as an element of its present meaning.

This problematisation of recorded meaning is present in the text as an effect. It interferes with memory. Any attempt at organisation made by the reader is temporary or, at best, conditional. The title, for example, does not precede the poem, but works within it along (for convenience) the poem's vertical and horizontal axis, as pause and as sequence. That is, the words 'Un Coup de Dés jamais n'abolira le hasard', differentiated by their own type-face, run through the poem as a broken statement, held in suspension. It ends two whole pages before the poem, so it is held over until the last words which begin to repeat 'Un Coup de Dés' in a different type-face, another register. The sequence is therefore not smooth or unidirectional. The title also punctuates the pages on which it appears because it is larger and heavier than the other type-faces, and it is always isolated to varying degrees by the white spaces. Each time the words appear, they recall the rest of the title at the same moment· as affording an apparent focus for the specific textual moment. The vertical axis is therefore deflected and dissipated by the introduction of the horizontal and its temporal movements back and forth. The basic pattern is repeated for the remaining six type-faces, making seven intersecting vertical and horizontal axes. These axes are also seven pivots, the whole articulating 'subdivisions prismatiques de l'idée', in the words of Mallarmé's preface. But they are impossible to retain *in toto* in the same way as the title may be retained, as a conscious and coherent proposition. They subsist in the memory as a fleeting complex of movements, and only subliminally as fragments of once-achieved meanings. These tend to repeat, so that meaning is concentrated and dissipated by turns, setting up a rhythm within the act of the reading of rapid influx of information and sudden loss. Forgetting is as much a part of reading as is remembering.

At the level of images, the effect is comparable, and the title is here again an active element, both abstract and representational. For example, let us take the title as representing the trajectory of the dice-throw, broken through the poem. It describes a line and is a physical gesture. The line is the basic component of written language, the stroke of the pen. This seems so literal that it is easy to dismiss, but meaning can be initiated by it, as I have tried to show. The line moves through the poem at all levels, as an abstract of writing, as memory-trace, on the basis of many of its metaphors, such as the wing, the plume, the waterspout, the hull of the boat, the cradle, the horizon, the waves, 'et en berce le vierge indice' (467).

To show the difference between the operation of the line in 'Un Coup de Dés' and earlier texts, and the effect on reading, let us look briefly at 'Soupir' which is similar enough to allow comparison, but which does not extend its visual *image* of a line to visual signification.

> Mon âme vers ton front où rêve, ô calme sœur,
> Un automne jonché de taches de rousseur,
> Et vers le ciel errant de ton œil angélique
> Monte, comme dans un jardin mélancolique,
> Fidèle, un blanc jet d'eau soupire vers l'Azur!
> – Vers l'Azur attendri d'Octobre pâle et pur
> Qui mire aux grands bassins sa langueur infinie
> Et laisse, sur l'eau morte où la fauve agonie
> Des feuilles erre au vent et creuse un froid sillon,
> Se traîner le soleil jaune d'un long rayon.   (39)

It would be possible to extract from the poem the simple statement 'Mon âme monte et laisse se trainer un long rayon'. There are three phrases beginning with 'vers' – line 1, line 3 and line 6 – each of which could apply to this movement: '[Mon âme] vers ton front . . . . . . vers le ciel errant de ton œil . . . [monte] – Vers l'Azur attendri d'Octobre . . .'. Strictly speaking, 'Octobre' is the subject of 'laisse', but because the verb 'monte' is suspended for three lines and because there are other finite verbs between subject, object and modifying phrases there is a hesitation or a moment's ambiguity which lingers. This is reinforced because the woman's features are confused with the landscape; her brow dreams autumn, her eye is the sky, which is reflected in the water. Finally the speaking voice of the poem is also merged because the motion of the soul is like the fountain. Thus far all these overlapping images are suggested through normal syntax. The passage in 'L'Après-Midi d'un Faune' which I looked at earlier (see pp. 48–9) is a refinement of this narcissistic projection and reflection, and it repeats the dream and the trace of the gaze – in 'Soupir', the cold furrow, in 'L'Après-Midi d'un Faune' the monotonous line. The refinement is considerable and 'L'Après-Midi d'un Faune' duplicates the reflection of the subject in its reference to language but nevertheless, the text still tries to stretch the resources of the linguistic code to make its meaning, both lexically and syntactically. In 'Un Coup de Dés' movements of this kind are developed beyond ambiguity and are foregrounded by means of irreconcilable breaks in syntax. Lay-out and typography work to propose a variety of syntactic relationships by visual means. On one level they are abstracts of the poem's spatial metaphors. But on the other levels they also initiate visual meaning. The trace of the gaze is still there in 'Un Coup de Dés'; the waterspout merging with the plume on the Hamlet-figure's hat and on the siren's brow. The poem is in the third person, however, and the line is intermittent. The poem takes all the earlier processes a step further by foregrounding the changes made in the language body. This is both its form and its subject-matter.

The constellation is another example of the poem's structural metaphors. It operates as an abstract of the poem's visual structure, and also of reading, in the way I have already described, as well as operating as a specific constellation, 'le Septentrion aussi Nord' (477). It therefore directs the reading towards the metaphors of a ship at sea in a storm, towards a different structural level and towards the reader's own activity. The construction of sense is therefore gradual. This makes further demands on the memory and extends the temporal reach of the poem. It is a radical change in the dynamics of reading, signifies a different economy of thought and requires a different kind of reading in which intense concentration and stimulation are succeeded by periods of greatly lowered awareness.

The visual in the poem, in this respect, is a kind of thought-pattern in which ideas are seen to form and re-form at different levels. It is the 'figure of a thought', as Valéry said,[7] but it is also a bodily gesture, the minimal sign of the energies suppressed in articulation. 'Un Coup de Dés' develops the latent visual structures of the earlier poems and in so doing is a radical innovation of the kind Mallarmé found in Manet and Impressionism. It foregrounds the changes made in the speaking subject and in the language body when new concepts are born, either small perceptions or great ideas. 'Un Coup de Dés' externalises and makes explicit the visual movements and spatial metaphors of earlier Mallarmé texts, and in this respect at least, it is clearer. Although the earlier poems and prose stretch syntactic structure, lexical boundaries and so forth, they contain their attempt to generate new meaning within language and, in the poems, within strict metrical form. In fact, this is tightened in the truncated sonnets which immediately preceded 'Un Coup de Dés'. By finally breaking away, the poem reaches the limit of what they could achieve, and it starts again.

In so doing it does more than cross the boundary between sense and non-sense. If this were all, it would be mere chaos – and the fear of chaos haunts the poem. It would also fail to innovate. In order to make a radical intervention, the text must indicate a new source of sense. In both the written and lithographic text, that source is in the multiplied relations between the Subject and language.

I have discussed the type of sign which combines an existential with a conventional relation between signifier and signified (see above, chapter 3). It is not difficult to see that a conventional relation between signifier and signified may be altered, because there is no necessary relation between them. But to alter an existential relation you have to make an internal change in either part of the sign, the signifier or the signified. This comes back to the body and text-body. The texts portray their own activity – in image and in structure – as a pantomimic or motor translation of the desired change. In so doing, they 'distort' the sign and the self-in-language, as may be seen in the grotesque drawing and in the graphemic activity of the layout and type-faces. It is important that these distortions are read as embodying desired change, not as withdrawal, or the deliberate evocation of fear. The fact that both may threaten is a sign of the repressive return of the law.

In this light we can see how the visual impact of 'Un Coup de Dés' is extended by the illustrations. The movement in language towards a fuller experience of reading is mirrored in lithographs which work in series, overlapping with each other and with the poem. 'Un Coup de Dés' repeats, overlaps. It does so internally. It also repeats other texts, the crisis of 'Igitur' and the re-invention of language in 'Hérodiade', the poem to which Mallarmé was returning at the end of his life. Hérodiade is a multiple figure, virgin princess gazing at her reflection in the mirror, in the nurse, 'pauvre aieule', and her own childhood. Igitur and Hérodiade are caught in their ancestral histories in an obsessive, hallucinatory and emotionally null state. Le Maître, ironically named, is projected on to them in his returns through his body's remembered impressions and desires. The poem is full of anxiety over lineage, descent, legacy, birth, trapped adolescence. The female presences of earlier poems are apparently erased. But not so. They are its environment, the mother-sea ('la mer', 'la mère') in which Le Maître struggles, his boat another suffocating womb.

> très à l'intérieur résume
>
> l'ombre enfouie dans la profondeur par cette voile alternative
>
>
> jusqu'adapter
> à l'envergure
>
> sa béante profondeur en tant que la coque
>
> d'un bâtiment   (461)

'coque' signifies a shell, cocoon or hull, the womb-like furrow in the waves or the treacherous vessel containing Igitur's projected idea in his game of chance, 'Le cornet est la Corne de licorne – d'unicorne' (441). The repetition of sound and shape of 'corne' in this line occurs in 'Un Coup de Dés' through the polysemy of individual words, which then form series of echoing shapes internally and with each other: 'l'envergure', the spread of the sail, wingspan; 'voile', sail, veil-mask-disguise, sail-boat; 'bâtiment', vessel, building, mother-symbol, (like 'nef' on the following page, which signifies a ship and the nave of a church). The external abyss repeats internally by means of all these imbrications, the reversal and recapitulation which begins with 'très à l'intérieur résume'. 'Cette voile alternative', like the wing which formerly hovered over the whiteness and expanse is now darkness telescoped 'l'ombre enfouie dans la profondeur'.

The sea-creature begins life, like the slow awakening of Redon's animal in *Les Origines* (fig. 42), and the animal's embryonic head also appears in the bottom quarter, together with the dice, and in the lithograph for 'Un Coup de Dés' with the child's head, above the arch (fig. 61). Knopff's illustration for 'À la nue accablante tue . . .' (fig. 68) is a constricted siren figure, twisted body, a rigid column at whose

68   Knopff, 'À la nue accablante tue . . .', 1895

feet is a shell into which she would have fitted with her bent head. Out of the shell emerges a second siren with a male child held against her body and following the same curve as the shell as if repeating the same figure in diminishing size. Redon's shrunken man (fig. 55) emerges from a tree which his body repeats. Siren-waterspout, tree-man, siren-shell, a continuum between figures and environment.

Hérodiade-mother-sea appears in the lithographs with Le Maître shrunk to a tiny creature clinging to her head in a foetal embrace, or just beginning to separate:

> dans ces parages
> > du vague   (475)

The shell-womb peels off from the top of the helmet ('Comme un casque guerrier d'impératrice enfant' 68). It follows the same curve, and at the bottom merges ambiguously into a sea-horse or fish-tail, or an ornamental part of the helmet. It is impossible to distinguish where the encased body ends and the helmet-head begins, or whether they divide at all. In the middle of the lithograph, before the woman's face and below the falling dice, there is a mask, half face, half melted dice:

> > > né
> > > > d'un ébat
> la mer par l'aieul tentant ou l'aieul contre la mer   (464)

As well as a mother–child union, the coupling is sexual:

Fiançailles

dont

le voile d'illusion rejailli leur hantise
ainsi que le fantôme d'un geste   (464)

The two figures are also part of the same individual. So, who, or what gives birth, and who or what is, or might be, born? Lover, mother, words; they are all recurrent throughout Mallarmé's poems as transformations of the hollow curve:

Sans fleurir la veillée amère
Le col ignoré s'interrompt.

Je crois que deux bouches n'ont
Bu, ni son amant ni ma mère
Jamais à la même chimère,
Moi, sylphe de ce froid plafond.   (74)

Mouth as shell, edifice, vagina:

Avance le palais de cette étrange bouche
Pâle et rose comme une coquillage marin.   (32)

Le temple enseveli divulgue par la bouche . . .
le gaz
. . . allume hagard un immortel pubis   (70)

Selon nul ventre que le sien
Filial aurait pu naître.   (74)

There is no shortage of poems in which Mallarmé's celebration and fear of the word-body and the female in himself may be read:

O la berceuse . . .
. . . accueille une horrible naissance   (40)

Hollow vessels . . . in these texts the repetition is perhaps more a scansion, because nothing stays the same (just read that last clause both ways!); in the lithographs, each figure is on the point of metamorphosis: the woman turns into the man, turns into the woman; her face sloughs off a skin-mask, his tail has two forms; the siren bursts out of its reptilian casing; the child's face begins to repeat itself outside its containing arch. Igitur's dice-box, stuck on the same sound, but each time with a different prefix or suffix.:

Le corne-t est la Corne de li-corne – d'uni-corne.   (441)

Une sonore vaine et monotone ligne   (51)

The hollow vessel is also a trumpet, 'le cornet':

À même les échos esclaves
Par une trompe sans vertu

Quel sépulcral naufrage . . .   (76)

'trompe', deceit, a terrible alliance of doubt and certainty, pulse and repulse:

> Toute Aurore même gourde
> A crisper un poing obscur
> Contre des clairons d'azur
> Embouchés par cette sourde
>
> A le pâtre avec la gourde
> . . .
> Tant que la source ample sourde   (72)

the rhymes reverse, meaning; 'gourde', numb, gourd; 'sourde', deaf, gush forth; 'obscur'/'azur', dark/light. Bringing our words, utterance fails to name:

> son site,
> . . .
> Ne porte pas de nom que cite
> L'or de la trompette d'Été.   (56)

> COMMENÇÂT-IL ET CESSÂT-IL
> sourdant que nié et clos quand apparu   (473)

Out of the hollow vessel, the spring, the sound, the trace of the idea projected in the dice:

> C'ÉTAIT
> issu stellaire   LE NOMBRE   (473)

The sequence of telescoping and scattering meaning, initiated by movement, shape and sound, starts again. Both the child and the siren are thrown up in 'cette conjonction suprême avec la probabilité:

> celui
> son ombre puérile
> caressée et polie et rendue et lavée
> assouplie par la vague et soustraite
> aux durs os perdus entre les ais   (464)

The universals of the sky, sea and stars figure the old man's physical being and mock his descent (lineage, fall). The waterspout:

> *plume solitaire éperdue*
>
> *cette blancheur rigide*
>
> *dérisoire*
> *en opposition au ciel*   (469)

   Igitur, Hamlet, 'prince amer de l'écueil' (469), in Mallarmé's essay on 'Hamlet' 'l'adolescent évanoui de nous aux commencements de la vie et qui hantera' (299), signifying 'la nostalgie de la prime sagesse inoubliée malgré les aberrations que cause l'orage battant la plume délicieuse de sa toque' (302). In 'Un Coup de Dés', there is no nostalgia about what the prince's 'toque de minuit' (469) might signify; 'toque', hat, mad (toqué), one letter, similar in sound-formation, away from 'coque'. There is an air of hysteria, 'un esclaffement sombre' (469). The next full page of the poem goes over the same ground, as the figure changes from prince to siren. In the lithograph (fig. 60) the gender of the emergent, winged siren-prince is indistinct. Mallarmé's Hamlet, 'fou en dehors . . . mais s'il fixe en dedans les yeux sur un image de soi qu'il y garde intacte autant qu'une Ophélie jamais noyée, elle! prêt toujours à se ressaisir.' (302) The internalised image of Ophelia comes closer to his self-image:

soucieux

   expiatoire et pubère

      muet

         rire

        que

        SI   (471)

the siren–prince is dumb, anxious. 'SI' in the same type as 'COMME SI' (466–7) the silent dangerous and hysterical vortex

au silence   *enroulée avec ironie*

          [. . .]

dans quelque proche   *tourbillon d'hilarité et d'horreur*   (466–7)

Laughter at the blockage-points, where a limit is encountered, a crisis.

The prince carries the waterspout on his head 'prince amer de l'écueil / s'en coiffe comme de l'héroïque' (469). What kind of a hero? Le Maître 'jadis il empoignait la barre' (463); a ship in a storm at sunset, the captain with his foot on a volcano:

de cette conflagration   à ses pieds

          de l'horizon unanime   (463)

What kind of a voyage is this? Mythic, as in other poems with the foot and the volcano?

M'introduire dans ton histoire
C'est en héros effarouché
S'il a du talon nu touché
Quelque gazon de territoire . . .

Comme mourir pourpre la roue
Du seul vespéral de mes chars.   (75)

Phaeton's chariot, yes, but whose story, whose history? The book is closed in another variant, 'Mes bouquins refermés sur le nom de Paphos':

Le pied sur quelque givre où notre amour tisonne,
Je pense plus longtemps peut-être éperdument
À l'autre, au sein brûlé d'une antique amazone.   (76)

Paphos, Aphrodite's island, the amazon. Mallarmé's translated accounts of the exploits of the gods, *Les Dieux Antiques*, stress their interchangeability: Oedipus cast into the sea in a box (1234ff.), like Dionysus or Perseus; Polynices' corpse burnt by Antigone, herself buried alive; Vulcan, spouse of Venus, his name deriving from the

Sanskrit for a torch or meteor (1201), leads to Achilles, 'Le Maître est allé puiser des pleurs au Styx' (68), who merges into Odysseus.

The echoes of a culture which wrote its history in myth sound strangely in 'Un Coup de Dés', which is not a universalising text. My aim in this reading has been to track some of the energies it may be read as trying to release. Many of these suppressed energies are female, as the text implicitly recognises and fears. Whether they are read as female because the female is suppressed in our culture, or whether we say they are suppressed because they are female is a difficult political question, and it is one which is raised by the text, if not in it. Mallarmé identifies with, and fears, the female as it extends into areas which are undervalued, disruptive or repressed, and into language and of course the female is elemental in both sexes, but the forms of cultural determination through which it is repressed are different in either sex. To read female meanings is therefore not a simple matter, and requires that we recognise this difference in 'Un Coup de Dés' and other texts. The birth theme is female and it operates in the text as individual, linguistic and cultural, that is to say, at every level.

In the next chapter I want to concentrate on the question of 'female' meanings and the presence of women in some of the texts I have looked at in this book.

5

GENDER-IN-SIGNIFICATION.

But there is no *invention* possible, whether it be philosophical or poetic, without the presence in the inventing subject of an abundance of the other ... I is the matter, personal, lively, exuberant, masculine, feminine, or other in which I delights me and distresses me.

Hélène Cixous and Catherine Clément. 'La jeune née'

Eau froide par l'ennui dans ton cadre gelée
Que de fois et pendant des heures, désolée
Des songes et cherchant mes souvenirs qui sont
Comme des feuilles sous ta glace au trou profond,
Je m'apparus en toi comme une ombre lointaine.

Mallarmé. 'Hérodiade'

Almost half Mallarmé's poems involve women in some explicit sense. They are constructed with a female presence at the centre (e.g. 'Apparition', 'Les Fleurs', 'Angoisse', 'Tristesse d'Été', 'Sainte', 'L'Après-Midi d'un Faune', 'Salut', 'À la nue ...'); contain a female persona, a 'sister' (e.g. 'Soupir', 'Don du Poème', 'Prose pour des Esseintes'); they are deflected off a woman's body (e.g. 'Une Négresse ...', 'Autre Éventail'); or they use the convention of the love sonnet (e.g. 'Dame / sans trop d'ardeur ...', 'O si chère de loin ...'). Many of the early poems are straightforward and conventional in this and other respects. This is not true of the later poems from 'Hérodiade' on, or of those which were extensively revised in the 1880s. Mallarmé usually stops short of ventriloquism; the women do not speak. 'Hérodiade' is an exception, perhaps because the relevant section is in dramatic form.

In this chapter I shall explore the tension in Mallarmé between textual and biological/social gender and aspects of the historical construction of gender-in-signification,[1] or the ways sexuality, creativity and the female body are made to work in the signifying process. The tension may clearly be seen, for example, in the convention of the love sonnet, which is shaped as a complex between the poet, his

69   Toorop, *The Three Brides*, 1893

70   Redon, *Des Esseintes*, 1882

persona as lover, his mistress and the public readership for which the poem was intended, which may or may not be predominantly women. The apparent address to women may be merely across women to men.

In Mallarmé's later poems women merge with the poetic process, partly through transference of his codes for poetry (whiteness, flight, light, potential utterance etc.) to women, and women's bodies (e.g. in the triptych 'Tout orgueil . . . ', 'Surgi de la croupe . . . ', 'Une dentelle . . . '). This transference exemplifies the slippage that often occurs between the woman and other meanings. It is a process that may be read as eradicating the woman, and this is often the case. But it may also open up the 'female' as a complex site of meaning which may be read as centering women. Part of this chapter will be about problems of reading the female signifiers in the texts but I shall also look at an example, Sollers's reading of Dante in the nineteenth century, of the way they may be appropriated as a sign, and relate his reading to Mallarmé.

In the opening line of the dramatic section of 'Hérodiade', the old nurse/confidant speaks to the princess:

> Tu vis! ou vois-je ici l'ombre d'une princesse?   (44)

Her words immediately connect seeing with life; 'vis', 'vois' are phonetically close, they are one phoneme apart and in these lines they have a paranomasic connection, since 'vis' puns on the present tense of 'to live' and the past historic of 'to see'. It is one of the ways of constructing a dense texture of meaning that often occurs in the Mallarmé text, especially where the voice is concerned, where the relation between senders and receivers of the message within the text and outside it (between text and text, text and reader) is somehow at play. 'Tu vis', furthermore, is both syntactically differentiated from the rest of the line and part of it. It is part exclamation, part question, discrete in its intransitive meaning (you live! do you live?) or sharing the same direct object in its transitive form 'Did you see, do I see, the shade/shadow of a princess?' 'Of a princess' fragments Hérodiade still further, splitting her self from her role or social rank as well as from her past self and her reflection.

'Hérodiade' is a poem, a female figure, a locus for Mallarmé's struggle with language. 'Hérodiade' as we know it was substantially written in 1864 and 1867, and it was a breakthrough in Mallarmé's 'invention of a language'. But it was never finished, and he was working on it again when he died. In other words its presence spans his mature work. It is characteristic of its time as an 'image of women'. But more importantly it shows something of Mallarmé's address in relation to women as signifiers in male history, and how this crosses his self-observation in language.

Writing to a friend, Eugène Lefébure, Mallarmé describes his totally new, 'pure' work, 'Hérodiade', as follows, and defines the modern poet as working with metalanguage:

C'est bien ce que je m'observe sur moi – je n'ai créé mon œuvre que par élimination, et toute vérité acquise ne naissait que de la perte d'une impression . . . hier j'ai fini la première ébauche de l'œuvre . . . Je l'ai contemplée sans extase comme sans épouvante, et, fermant les yeux, *j'ai trouvé que cela était*. La

'Vénus de Milo' – que je me plais à attribuer à Phidias, tant le nom de ce grand artiste est devenu générique pour moi, 'la Joconde' du Vinci, me semblent, et *sont* les deux grands scintillations de la Beauté sur cette terre – et cette Œuvre telle qu'elle est rêvée, la troisième. La Beauté complète et inconsciente, unique et immuable, ou la 'Vénus de Phidias', la Beauté ayant été mordue au cœur depuis le christianisme par la Chimère, et douleureusement renaissant avec un sourire rempli de mystère, mais de mystère forcé et qu'elle *sent* être la condition de son être. La Beauté enfin, ayant par la science de l'homme, retrouveé dans l'Univers entier ses *phases corrélatives*, ayant eu le suprême mot d'elle, s'étant rappelé l'horreur secrète qui la forçait à sourire – du temps du Vinci, et à sourire mystérieusement – souriant mystérieusement maintenant, mais de bonheur et avec la quiétude éternelle de la 'Vénus de Milo' retrouvée ayant su l'idée du mystère dont 'la Joconde' ne savait que la sensation fatale.[2]

A great deal could be said about this as a version of 'Hérodiade'. The contrast between the Mona Lisa and the Venus de Milo is perennial.[3] The passage will perhaps recall Baudelaire's stanza on Da Vinci, in 'Les Phares'.

> . . . miroir profond et sombre,
> Où des anges charmants, avec un doux souris
> Tout charge de mystère . . .

or Walter Pater, writing some five years later in *The Renaissance*, and his vampiric Mona Lisa, 'expressive of what in the ways of a thousand years men had come to desire.' It would appear to fit into the 'Sacred and Profane' version of 'Symbolism',[4] especially in painting, which is typified by J.-K. Huysmans both in *À Rebours* (the novel whose central character, des Esseintes, popularised the 'decadent hero') and in his art criticism. Whatever such accounts might clarify, there is far too much they cannot account for. The same is true of far more sophisticated and recent histories, which have otherwise much to offer.

Seeking ways of accounting for the 'surgissement archéologique' of Dante's texts in the nineteenth century, Philippe Sollers interrogates their contradictory appearances, as invisible as Sade, yet endowed with a formal presence he calls Homeric, on the level of language and writing, 'le rapport profond que Dante entretient avec l'écriture'.[5] In this, Beatrice is read as the sign of Dante's non-identity, not some idealised historical figure of Beatrice, nor as an allegorical Woman. According to Sollers, Woman as sign is 'le lieu de la loi (de la réproduction), et en même temps elle détient le pouvoir matériel (biologique) d'en reconnaître la transgression'.[6] As a strategy and as a reading of mythic 'presences' in the nineteenth century and now, Sollers also opens out the question of gender as it functions in the text – and, as such, as the conjunction of meanings, representations of the subject, as suture. But Beatrice remains, in this account, a representation of Woman in a way that Dante is not of Man, because her body is implicated differently – as sign and as her only speech. Mallarmé, in the letter I have just quoted, genders his still unarticulated work female, the third image to stand with the Venus and the Mona Lisa. 'Œuvre', 'Beauté', 'l'Univers', all feminine nouns, man's science one by one, 'ayant eu le suprême mot d'elle'. He does the same again in 'The Impressionists and Edouard Manet' in trying to locate the 'mental operation' demanded in Impressionism:

Those persons much accustomed . . . to fix on a mental canvas the beautiful remembrance of woman, even when thus seen amid the glare of night in the world or at the theatre, must have remarked that some mysterious process despoils the noble phantom of the artificial prestige cast by candelabra or footlights, before she is admitted fresh and simple to the number of every day haunters of the imagination. (73–4)

Sollers finds that Beatrice's loss of identity (as a historical figure) is the sign of Dante's non-identity, 'l'espace où se déploie son écriture comme désir, son désir comme écriture indéfinie.'[7] Beatrice is eradicated while Dante's negation is reversed. The process Sollers describes is accurate, but he does nothing to counter it in his inscription of these historical scenarios into present and contemporary language. In both Sollers and Mallarmé there is a variable, unannounced process of shifting realities and conflation of terms. While claiming a kind of constancy of 'Woman-as-sign', free transferences between levels of textual activity occur to erase the links between utterance and contexture at the moment they are proposed, 'elle' (whatever 'elle' may signify) 's'efface enfin dans l'écriture qu'elle suscite'.[8] As in the fairy story retold by Freud, the solution is bought at the cost of the sister's dumbness.[9]

At this point the question of historical gender-in-articulation, generation of meaning and the visual intersect. Staying with the same intertextuality, between Mallarmé, the myth of Dante and Beatrice in the nineteenth century, and Sollers, how do we question the association of the woman with the specular in the construction of the imaginary? And how do we avoid being limited by sexed identity without saying that the gender of the individual writer (present or past) has no functional effect; all these as informing the 'new problematic of the imaginary' outlined above and moving towards possible readings across texts whose thrust is transgressive of the visual–aural divide in signification. The question of gender and of the elements of signification, minimal or introversive semiosis, overlap at critical points. Sollers crosses from what he calls the maternal language ('langue', mother tongue, born through the mother from which he derives) of prohibition to vision 'à l'inverse d'Œdipe'. Beatrice is at this point opposed also to Eurydice.

À la parole aveugle de l'antiquité se substitute une transgression délibérée, un avènement et une consommation de la vue (dans la *Comédie*, une fois disparue la langue paternelle – Virgile – dans la renaissance d'un langage innocent échappant à la loi, Béatrice oblige à Dante à la regarder et à lui parler, elle le fait se retourner sur le chemin parcouru, vers la terre, elle s'efface enfin dans l'écriture qu'elle suscite.)[10]

At the resolution of the Œdipus complex, the moment of entry into culture, the woman becomes the currency, the means of exchange, a facilitating and empty signifier. Thus she is (again 'she' as female gender, woman, the linguistic feminine) both death and desire, innocence and transgression.

> Une dentelle s'abolit
> Dans de doute du Jeu suprême
> À n'entr'ouvrir comme un blasphème

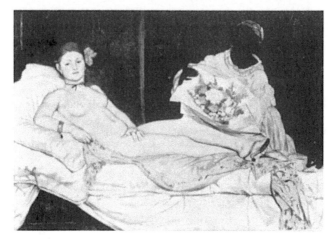

71 Manet, *Olympia*, 1863

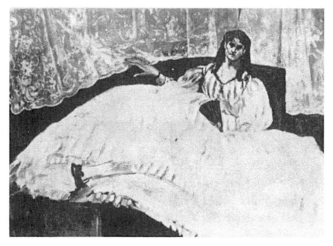

72 Manet, *Portrait of Jeanne Duval*, c.1862

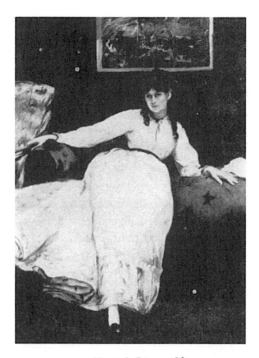

73 Manet, *Le Repos*, c.1869

Qu'absence éternelle de lit.

. . .

Telle que vers quelque fenêtre
Selon nul ventre que le sien,
Filial on aurait pu naître.   (74; cf. figs. 72–4)

Mallarmé's Venus and Mona Lisa are still there as oppositions.

The Œdipus myth is overlaid with the Orpheus and Eurydice myth, the two conflated into the Freudian cultural myth. The incest taboo, with its apparent biological imperative – the inward focus of familial relations has to be countered, powerful bonds transferred for the good of the species over the individual – dissolves into the Orphic at several possible points, exile, death, prohibition, the look and, like Virgil giving way to Beatrice, the philosophical mysteries of Orphism are overlaid with Christianity. Dante's medieval cosmology, and poetic utterance is, in its most distilled form, as litany. 'Mystère, autre que représentatif et que, je dirai, grec, Pièce, office' – writing a little before 'Un Coup de Dés', Mallarmé probes religious ritual while seeking some secular location for *jouissance*, 'l'archaïque outremer des ciels' (393), the source, creation.

If indeed, in the *Divine Comedy* Beatrice cancels herself in the 'écriture' to which she gives birth ('suscite'), the other to Mallarmé's gaze does not. In *Le Nénuphar blanc* Mallarmé's first person narrator seeks out, 'les yeux au-dedans fixés sur l'entier oubli d'aller', his neighbour 'l'inconnue à saluer'.

'Sûr, elle avait fait de ce cristal son miroir intérieur à l'abri de l'indiscretion éclatante des après-midi; elle y venait et la buée d'argent glaçant des saules ne fût bientôt que la limpidité de son regard habitué à chaque feuille'.   (284)

The delicacy of this prose-poem, like his delight in textures, fans, is an aspect of Mallarmé's writing that has proved as difficult to reconcile with the cosmic dramatist as the bourgeois ladies of Impressionism have with the Salomés (see figs. 5–7 and 72–4) the mythical scale and portentous tone of the 'Symbolists'. But there is no such separation in Mallarmé's vocabulary or address in relation to language from the most trivial-seeming forms upwards, as in 'Une dentelle s'abolit' the lace pattern merges into the supreme game. This is far-reaching because it concerns the whole primary–secondary, absolute–relative, self–other, active–passive, past–present, unconscious–conscious, female–male – all the oppositions and inversions which hover implicit in the multiform contradictions these texts seem to present, and the elusive power that derives from them. Why, in short, they work when they are supposed to suffer from such flaws as superficiality or perverse obscurity.

Derrida argues, in *Signs and the Blink of an Eye*,[11] that the possibility of re-presentation, the constitution of a trace must be allowed both to inhabit and to constitute the now. The internal presence of non-presence (Beatrice in Dante, Hérodiade as virgin in Mallarmé) and otherness would confirm the necessity of signs to the self-relation. The phenomenological arguments about time-consciousness which are of importance to understanding the Impressionism Mallarmé began to work out, extend into those of signification. The exploration of the perceptual moment implicates expressive form and the self-relation. Derrida acknowledges that the problem of this relationship between retention and re-presentation is the same as that of the history of 'life' and life's becoming conscious. To construct a sign which straddles the frontier between present and non-present touches the whole economy of relations around the Œdipal moment, the castration complex which patriarchy describes in terms which distort both the nature of difference and of primordial relations, including the sexual. From then the pairs of opposites are conflated – in psychoanalysis: 'the active–passive dichotomy is prior to the subsequent oppositions between phallic and castrated, masculine and feminine, which eventually subsume it', consolidating the whole separation between primary and secondary processes, and the logic of affectivity and reason.[12]

It is not easy to find ways of understanding the status of gender (or of address, or of 'The look') in nineteenth-century iconography. The transformations between the recurrent myths in the end are fairly restricted, despite their eclecticism. Myths deriving from Shakespeare, Dante, or the Greek Classics require to be read against Courbet, Manet, Whistler, Gauguin, because in their foregrounding of an experiential formal structure they implicate the receiver of the message more clearly. By so doing they particularly constitute a challenge. I, as a female subject, have the space to intervene.

It is possible to read the texts as posing the question of gender-in-signification at the same time as that of internalised non-presence because the female is often emptied of signification, as I have said, and this creates the space for new meanings. In his review of the ballet, Mallarmé progressively writes the woman out of the dance. But this is not all he does. He also writes the poet out of the poem, and initiates a sense of the marvellous, 'par le prodige de reccourcis ou d'élans'; the sign telescopes *or* takes flight. Any prose attempt to emulate the process would require dialogue. By moving out of the poem, the poet sets up an interchange as he does with the female, the 'other', the overall movement being concentrated in the body – of the dancer-sign and the poem-sign:

À savoir que la danseuse *n'est pas une femme qui danse*, pour ces motifs juxtaposés qu'elle *n'est pas une femme*, mais une métaphore résumant un des aspects élémentaires de notre forme, glaive, coupe, fleur, etc., et *qu'elle ne danse pas*, suggérant, par le prodige de raccourcis ou d'élans, avec une écriture corporelle ce qu'il faudrait des paragraphes en prose dialoguée autant que descriptive, pour exprimer, dans la rédaction: poème dégagé de tout appareil du scribe.   (304)

Mallarmé's disengagement of the dance-poem from the dancer and the poem leaves the moving body as the minimal signifier, close to the point of invariance.

As with the use of 'ptyx' in 'Ses purs ongles' as an empty signifier (see chapter 3), the dancer's body is a sign at the pivot between meaninglessness and total meaning. It is embodiment and disembodiment at the same time, and the dual pulse, 'raccourcis, élans', sounds from the smallest units of the sign-body to the whole. As in the formula 'le langage peut se contenter de l'opposition de quelquechose avec

74   Whistler, *Studies of Loie Fuller dancing*, n.d.

rien', the sign-body has a certain autonomy. At this level, too, there is a gender imbalance in the capacity to make meaning. The masculine can have zero signification, whereas the feminine, at present, cannot; by articulating a feminine noun, you limit the gender, whereas the masculine is either male or inclusive, or non-gender-specific. Moreover, the feminine has zero morphological function, so that in using it you also convey less grammatical information. But such semiotic limits are potentially opened up by the movements in these texts, not least because the specific language-event is displaced from its privileged role in signification and in cognition:

> Si de mon sein pas du sien
> A jailli le sanglot pire   (66)

The song bird of 'Petit Air II' inhabits a space like the dancer's, the poet's internalised non-presence, the elusive sign held on to by playing on a single unit of meaning, the reversal of 'sein-sien', crossing the body boundaries within the sign.

Where the female is involved in this process there is frequently in Mallarmé texts – and to some extent in Redon and Manet – a strong identification with the female body in the sender of the message. Rather than portraying it, the text makes its addresses through it. This can be either direct or a kind of birth. In 'Don du Poème', the poet–father brings his gift, couched in terms of the forbidden traditions of cabbalistic ritual, reaching back to the legend of Esau's disinheritance, to frame its account of the beginning, of life and of articulation. He approaches the mother and daughter as a new father in a domestic situation (as Mallarmé himself was):

O la berceuse, avec ta fille et l'innocence
De vos pieds froids   (40)

and the mother is sought as a mythic goddess, Bhavâni from whose milk the Ocean
of causes formed:

Avec le doigt fané presseras-tu le sein
Par qui coule en blancheur sibylline la femme
Pour les lèvres que l'air du vierge azur affame?

In *La Tentation de Saint Antoine*, (which Redon transposed three times) Flaubert told
the story as one of the saint's visions, a temptation, again of a kind of birth, this time
from a male body. The god Hari 'jeune, imberbe, plus beau qu'une fille' reclines on a
lotus leaf, with a lotus flower growing out of his navel. Out of this were born the
three deities, Brahma (the creator), Ŝiva (the destroyer) and Vishnu (the preserver).

75   *Hari and Vishnou*, from Kreuzer's *Hindu Gods*

77   Kupka, *The Beginning of Life*, c.1900

76   *Bhavani* or *Ganga*, from
Kreuzer's *Hindu Gods*

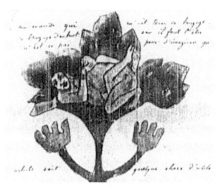

78   Gauguin, sketch from *Noa Noa*, 1893

The bodies and the earth, plants and gods are continuous matter. Mallarmé's Western paternal poet approaches his domestic Madonna with little hope that their culture can begin to accommodate this desire, in its fullness. Self-creation in 'Don du Poème' is bitter and defeated. In 'À la nue accablante tue . . .' it is constricted and empty at once. Knopff's illustration (fig. 68) of the poem, as we have already seen, transposes its tension and enclosure into the siren's body, where the distorted neck and head float above the swirls of cloud-hair and column-body. The body is divided, while at her feet, from a shell, it is multiplied.

Just as these transformations occur in the painting, so they may be seen in other poets. For example, in Laforgue's 'Complainte du Foetus du Poète' the language-body addresses the same questions of primal self-making, with its danger of destruction of identity and the capacity to make meaning. Meaning regresses to the minima, the body to the foetus

> . . . bavant,
> Dodo à les seins dorloteurs des nuages

close to the child's first separation from its physical and social environment

> Vous, Madame, allaitez le plus longtemps possible
> Et du plus seul de vous ce pauvre enfant-terrible

from the breast and in verbal communication. And nearly absurd, as in Mallarmé's 'Aboli bibelot d'inanité sonore', meaningless alternations, but taking pleasure in their rhythmic noise. Laforgue's foetus contracts

> Au pays de vin viril faire naufrage!
> Courage,
> Là, là, je me dégage . . .
> — et je communerai, le front vers l'Orient.

The mother figure, the East, and the sun all seem to be located at this juncture between undifferentiation, separation and meaning. If the poem gives birth to a self-in-language, it does so across gender, and cultures and across signs. It has or it desires the capacity to alter the physical and the language-body, not synchronously, or along the same axes or levels of symbolisation and relation to reality, but to make them cross at the point of meaning. There would seem to be two basic relations here, between the body and other bodies and between the body and the environment, taking 'body' as both the textual (linguistic or visual) and the physical. In these texts, the female as endowed with the capacity for self-renewal in the daughter (mother in this restricted sense) can extend her body into the outside, changing both itself and the social fabric. The processes of introjection and incorporation, the one psychic and the other physical, meet in the gesture of making the sign.

In Manet, this use of the body as signifier (ostension) between the physical and sign-body is recurrent, as we have to some extent seen in *Un Bar aux Folies Bergères* (fig. 34) and its presentation. Two, or is it three, figures perhaps at the moment of transaction: the female looking towards and away from the male and from the spectator, us, as receiver of the message, if such there be. There is an outward direction, but it does not prevail, even though the space is so public. The balcony, formally repeating the counter, is a stage-set, with the figures using their bodies to signify, assisted by their costume. Mallarmé's dancer figure, whose body writes, but then who has no body and no writing, posed the same question of gender-in-signification, where the opposition of something with nothing has to be made. In both the mask is assumed, the body boundary dissolved in broken touches or repeated figures, pantomimic movements, discontinuities and distortions, projections and introjections: all rituals to engender meaning.

In *Un Déjeuner sur l'Herbe* (fig. 8) a ritual meal where oppositions propose in a witty phantasm, the scale and spatial strangeness dislodge the symmetry of the figures, and the details distract the attention. Meaning is not invested in the man who makes the gesture but in the arrangement of bodies and their varying degrees of undress and disguise. The power relationships within the painting are by no means simple, and this is significant in terms of internal structure and of textual address.

It will be evident that I do not experience most of the texts I have discussed which depict woman as voyeuristic. I have heard *Un Déjeuner sur l'Herbe* criticised because it shows a naked woman and a partially clad woman in the company of two fully dressed men. But objection on these grounds is only valid if it takes account of how the power relations between them and with the spectator are inscribed and how the body and clothing are made to signify. The women in this text occupy a very different space from that of a conventional nude, and for many reasons. For example, the realism of the naked woman and the assertiveness of her look and her pose are a challenge to convention, and so is the way codes of depiction are problematised through the construction of the space occupied by the second female figure. The pile of clothes mixed with the food spilling out of a basket is like the props in Manet's etching of Polichinelle, where the clown's head bursts through a vaginal slash in the curtain-wall, a stage-set with a painting hung on it (fig. 38). The hat and sword further relay to other paintings of Manet's, such as *Mlle Victorine dressed as an Espada* (not illustrated), the same model as in *Un Déjeuner sur l'Herbe* (fig. 8), wearing ritual male bullfighting gear. Victorine herself, her face as clearly recognisable in these paintings as in her mask-like portrait, indicates a set of relationships between paired bodies in the paintings and in mental constructs. *Olympia* (fig. 71) looks away from the Black woman bearing flowers, a secret vagina, speaking another message, like Mallarmé's Black woman in 'Une négresse . . .':

> Et, dans ses jambes ou la victime se couche,
> Levant une peau noire ouverte sous le crin,
> Avance le palais de cette étrange bouche
> Pâle et rose comme un coquillage marin.   (31)

In this early poem the woman and the girl-child ('une enfant', 'la victime') mingle their bodies as if the child is ingested or perhaps in a symbiotic relationship: 'sous leur robe trouée', under their dress, which they seem to share, the child is already filled with guilty fruit, 'triste de fruits nouveaux / Et criminels aussi', while later the woman laughs 'de ses dents naïves à l'enfant'. Breasts and belly are compared, without indication of whose they are, 'À son ventre compare heureuses deux tétines', as if, like the dress, they are undifferentiated in body. Mallarmé's Faune is closer still to the twinned women,

> Mon crime, c'est d'avoir, gai de vaincre ces peurs
> Traîtresses, divisé la touffe echevelée
> De baisers que les dieux gardainent si bien melée. (52)

In these texts, the 'female' is not the old ideal, disengaged from social reality. It is rather the opposite, since it is focusing the sign itself, leading directly to the levels where meaning is produced. As the textual activity explores its own processes, exclusions, historical articulation, it crosses the female and male Subject as it is constructed through them. Though the activity of the text is reflexive, its energy is outwardly directed and engages with the problem of how cultural norms exert their repressive power.

It seems to me that historical analysis needs to take account at all levels of these different discourses of sexuality and power, and recognise how gender works as a determinant of textual production both as regards the producer and the message. The most common counter-argument I have come across to statements of this kind is based on class with which gender is supposedly comparable. This is a false and muddling opposition. The way that gender might be analysed as operating at the level of the production of meaning would seem to require a very different framework from that adopted by the advocates of this position. Most women can only be inserted into current analyses of class if they are defined in relation to the men who are recognised as producers. Women as producers, the female as productive, otherwise remain marginal.

6

CONCLUDING NOTE
A NEW CONCEPTION OF THE REAL

> Affres du passé nécessaires
> Agrippant comme avec des serres
> Le sépulcre de désaveu.
>
> Mallarmé. 'Tout Orgueil fume-t-il du soir'

That this rupture can be complicity with the law or, rather, that it can constitute a point of departure for even deeper changes: that is the major problem.

Hélène Cixous. 'Sorties'[1]

> Avec comme pour langage
> Rien qu'un battement aux cieux
> Le futur vers se dégage
> Du logis très précieux.
>
> Mallarmé. 'Éventail'

I began with a specific historical and formal question concerning the nature of the visual in Mallarmé's innovatory language and how it relates to the changes brought about in painting by contemporaries, especially those who worked with him. The relation between the visual and the aural sign, and what it can tell us about innovation, therefore underlies all my explorations, whether within language, within painting, or between the two. The reasons why this area has been less well understood than it might be and why it is becoming more accessible are connected with wider issues.

A shift of attention has been required towards reading textual innovation in terms of the function of signs in the continuing process of their own construction and that of the self as social construct. This shift implies revising our conception of the real in terms of the dynamic between meanings, existing and potential. Such a resituation is strategic and signifies (among other things) the restoration of links between art practice, critical practice and social reality.

My analyses have been informed by this. What does it mean to say – to take again my basic question – that the word and the image are not oppositions and they can change each other? It may be worth elaborating this a little here, since it summarises structures common to the fundamental arguments in this book. One of the productive features of the relationship as it appears in Mallarmé, Manet and Redon concerns the nature of the real, because the word and image stand in what appears to be a contradictory relation to the real. The image connects directly with perceptual reality because it either has an existence as an object or derives its existence from a percept. Unlike the word, the image is never totally arbitrary or abstract. But the word is only arbitrary at one level and the image is not tied, in the system of signs, to its referent. I say 'referent' because the initiating percept is neither exactly signifier nor signified, if for no other reason than that it exists or part exists outside the semiotic system and the imaginary.

In conceptual reality, this relationship between word, image and the real, changes. The change is particularly visible in the texts where they operate on the borders between the pre-conscious and the conscious where the word, the object and the image are not clearly differentiated. Reaching back from the word to the image-concept can extend the range of what is perceptible. The child gratifies its wishes through hallucinatory objects. The ritual object has transgressive power. With differences, clearly, material change can be effected in and through the sign and its relation to the thing (object and image). I am not saying there is no such thing as delusion. One feature of delusion, for example, would be to transfer the laws of one system directly to the other, eradicating the transitional movements which appear as distortions. The 'transition', moreover, is not a stage in the passage from one state to another, but essential to the system. The changes in time and space are not synchronous or total in the reality these texts present. This has a significant effect on the kinds of coherence they constitute. As the relation between time and space changes – and the basic distinction between the visual and the aural sign is between time and space – the formation of coherence is at the same time a break. The actual change may be minute, but what that signifies may be vast:

> Telles, immenses, que chacune
> Ordinairement se para
> D'une lucide contour, lacune,
> Qui des jardins la sépara. (56)

Part of the problem of recognising the relative scale of the initial and the subsequent change is how we accommodate the immanent into meaning and the effect this has on our conceptions of reality. I have tried to show how this is traceable in textual movements betweeen word and object and image and in textual effects such as the apparent objective space from which the message seems to come. This effect derives at least partly from the promotion of factors in human communication that we marginalise or under-value. No doubt there are some we do not even see at all yet.

Since the texts re-present the real (both as objects and as social relations) through the sign-system, meaning is produced both at the levels of relation to external reality and to the internal reality of the sign-system itself. As they do not differentiate between these realities they do not prioritise either of them. Both realities, as we have seen, also share the dimension, internal in another sense, of the spectator's Subjectivity. We have also seen that where the texts may seem not to refer, they may still signify because the refusal at one level or in one dimension of reality may open another, as when they shift between percept and concept.

In the texts I have analysed in this book, these transferences occur most clearly in Redon, partly because he uses the language of the visionary which signals in an immediate way that some kind of changed relation between internal and external is involved. But I find the novelty of his message less clear without knowledge of Manet's, because of the shift of emphasis towards ordinary, external reality, in terms of concern with perception and also with subject-matter, in which Manet made a clear move from the pre-constituted sign-system towards the mental and social realities for which that system had become inadequate. There is in both Manet and Redon a dual pulse in which connotation is denied and asserted, now at the level of the system, now at that of the subject. The same is true of Mallarmé. Connotation at either level overlaps so that the texts are shot through with contradictions, signs not of their own failure but of the structure of the real. They are more comprehensible together, not because they are in some sense incomplete, but because of the moves the spectator has to make to see their coherence.

The search for coherence and meaning is not a return to 'classicism' or a denial of 'modernism'.[2] But to dispense with the attempt to understand the drive of the texts towards a new kind of coherence and clarity would be a dangerous luxury. So would refusing to relate them to present, recognisable reality. If the texts operate at the site of the production of meaning, they *risk* dissolution into a mass of floating signifiers, rather than seek it. De-hierarchisation, which is one of the features I have tried to indicate, dissolves single meanings as surely as it does those structures which depend on them and on clear hierarchies, such as ambiguity.

If in the process of transmutation as I have described it, the Subject is fragmented, then so is the Other. The texts that break up pre-constituted meanings do not have to begin with the dominant. As marginalised meanings and those of the dominated change on a large scale, they take with them the meanings of the dominant and central. The fact that we are gaining more understanding of how the whole cultural production of a period participates in generating meaning helps in the work of allowing full weight to the presence of a multiplicity of 'movements' as a signifier in itself, and of analysing what this means to the female and the male Subject. My attention to the alterations in the visual and the aural sign has been aimed at relating formal structures to experience and to reality. This problem, together with the historical problems of resituating women as producers of meaning in texts written by men, as well as those by women with which other feminist critics are currently engaged, has motivated my study with equal strength and its ostensible subject-area. They are of course still in need of much fuller expression, but this is the direction and the territory I have wished to help make accessible by concentrating on transformations between repressed and non-rational meanings and their opposites, because unless their interdependence is understood the coherence of textual articulation of the repressed remains fragmented. Women's meanings up to the present are different from men's, and though they may coincide in details, cross and re-cross, because their structural location is not the same, they never exactly merge. They may have more in common, structurally, with the meanings of other cultures, so freely plundered in the nineteenth century, and with outlawed, or supposedly insane, experience. Women's meanings are both separate from, and integral to, the cultural whole. We need to understand how that contradiction may be made to work productively.

APPENDIX

LIST OF ILLUSTRATIONS, WITH NOTES

Illustrations are placed either where first mentioned; or where the most detailed reference is made; or to form a series with other paintings.

Fig. 1   Edouard Manet. *Portrait of Mallarmé*. Oil. 1876. Louvre.

Fig. 2   Gustave Courbet. *Portrait of Baudelaire*. Oil. c. 1847. Montpellier-Musée Fabre. 'but about 1860 a sudden and lasting light shone forth when Courbet began to exhibit' Mallarmé, 'The Impressionists and Edouard Manet' (66). Of Baudelaire, Mallarmé wrote, 'These strange pictures' (by Manet) 'at once won his sympathy . . . before their prompt succession and the sufficient exposition of the principles they inculcated had revealed their meaning' (67). Notice the similarity of the hand in fig. 25.

Fig. 3   Manet. *Le Linge*. Oil. 1876. Barnes Foundation. Mallarmé focussed his discussion of technique and 'plein air' on this painting. 'His truly marvellous work, this year refused by the Salon, but exhibited to the public by itself . . . – a work which marks a date in a lifetime perhaps, but certainly one in the history of art'. ('The Impressionists and Edouard Manet' 72.) Linen, whiteness and associated words became a theme in Mallarmé's writing, as metaphor for the page, as a joke in his letters to Whistler about publishing his address-quatrains (See Mallarmé *Œuvres* 81–106) in an illustrated volume, *Les Loisirs de la Poste*; see Barbier, *Correspondance Mallarmé–Whistler*.

Fig. 4   Courbet. *Le Sommeil*. Oil. 1866. Petit Palais.

       J'accours; quand à mes pieds, s'entrejoignent (meurtries

       De la langeur goutée à ce mal d'être deux)

       Des dormeuses parmi leur seuls bras hasardeux;

       Je les ravis, sans les désenlacer . . . Mallarmé. 'L'Après-midi d'un Faune.'

Courbet's works, according to Mallarmé, 'in some degree coincided with that movement which had appeared in literature, and which obtained the name of Realism; that is to say, it sought to impress upon the mind by the lively depiction of things as they appeared to be, and vigorously excluded all meddlesome imagination.' ('The Impressionists and Edouard Manet', 68.)

Fig. 5   Regnault. *Salomé*. Oil. 1871. Metropolitan Museum of Art, New York. Henri Regnault was a childhood friend of Mallarmé's, killed in action at Bugenval in the Franco-Prussian War. Mallarmé wrote an article about him and mentioned him in 'The Impressionists and Edouard Manet'. Henri Cazalis, the mutual friend to whom Mallarmé wrote many of his most revealing letters of the 1860s, including those about 'Hérodiade', wrote a book about Regnault, *Henri Regnault, sa vie et son œuvre*.

Fig. 6   Moreau. *Fleur Mystique*. Oil. c. 1875. Musée Gustave Moreau.

Fig. 7   Puvis de Chavannes.*Beheading of John the Baptist*. Oil. 1869. The Barber Institute of Fine Arts, the University of Birmingham. Puvis's paintings are all philosophical and they are largely, though not exclusively, classical in derivation and structure as opposed to the medievalism of the Pre-Raphaelites.

The following six were all mentioned in 'The Impressionists and Edouard Manet' as marking further stages in his development of a new art.

Fig. 8   Manet. *Un Déjeuner sur l'Herbe*. Oil. 1863. Louvre. Another very controversial painting, for the same reasons as *Olympia*. Furthermore, its subject is a kind of phantasm, on the dividing line between contemporary reality, myth and private fantasy; its spaces, groupings and perspective are strange, and the ironic or indifferent expressions on the people's faces challenge the spectator.

Fig. 9   Manet. *Le Bon Bock*. 1873. Private collection.

Fig. 10   Manet. *L'Exécution de l'Empereur Maximilien*. 1867. Städische Kunsthalle Mannheim. For a detailed account of this painting, see Sandblad *E. Manet*. In addition to doing several preparatory studies, Manet reworked it, cut up the canvas, repeated parts in other paintings (especially the soldier re-loading his rifle). It is one of the most explicitly political paintings Manet ever made, taking its subject and the details from newspaper accounts, but dressing the firing squad in French uniforms. This connects with his paintings of the barricades and with Goya's *3rd of May*. The soldier in the foreground, the peasants looking over the wall and the confusion around the three victims relate the public figure and event with the private and with a moment in the ordinary lives which it will affect in the political aftermath.

Fig. 11   Manet. *En Bateau*. Oil. 1874. Metropolitan Museum of Art, New York.

Fig. 12   Manet. *Argenteuil*. Oil. 1874. Museum of Fine Arts, Tournai, Belgium.

Fig. 13   Manet. *Le Balcon*. 1868–9. In 'The Impressionists and Edouard Manet', entitled *Des Gens du monde à la fenêtre*. Paris, Musée d'Orsay, Galerie du Jeu de Paume.

All three of the following were commented on by Mallarmé in 'Le Jury de Peinture pour 1874 et M. Manet' (see *Œuvres* 695–700).

Fig. 14   Manet. *Le Bal de l'Opéra*. Oil. 1873. Washington, National Gallery. 'Capital dans l'œuvre du peintre et y marquant comme un point culminant . . .' (697) 'Je ne crois pas qu'il y ait lieu de faire autre chose que de s'étonner de la gamme délicieuse trouvée dans les noirs . . . la couleur grave et harmonieuse que fait un groupe formé presque exclusivement d'hommes' (698).

Fig. 15   Manet. *Les Hirondelles*. Oil. 1873. Private collection. 'L'impression de plein air se fait jour d'abord; et ces dames, toutes à elles-mêmes . . . ne sont que des accessoires dans la composition' (698.)

Fig. 16   Manet. *Le Chemin de Fer*. Oil. 1873. Washington, National Gallery. 'Très singulier pour un œil d'amateur et doué d'une séduction calme.' The article is an ironic attack on the Jury system for the selection of paintings for the Salon (see Boime, *The Academy*). Mallarmé takes the accusation of lack of finish as one of the spurious criteria used against Manet. 'Qu'est-ce qu'une œuvre "pas assez poussée" alors qu'il y a entre tous ses éléments un accord par quoi elle se tient . . .' (698). The public has the right to see what the painter chooses to show, and to establish a direct relationship. 'Quant au public, arrêté, lui, devant la reproduction immédiate de sa personnalité multiple, va-t-il ne plus jamais détourner les yeux de ce miroir pervers . . .' (696). These basic points are developed into the historical analysis of 'The Impressionists and Edouard Manet', especially the defence of technical freedom and the social function of the artist in allowing 'the multitude' 'to see with its own eyes' and thus be placed 'directly in communion with the sentiment of their time' (84).

Figs. 17, 18, 19 and 20   Manet. 'L'Après-Midi d'un Faune'. 1876. Hand coloured woodcuts.

Fig. 21   Hokusai. *Lily*. Sketch from *Mangwa*. (Manet also drew a raven after Hokusai.)

The following six are all Manet's illustrations for Mallarmé's prose translation of Poe's poem 'The Raven'. Manet rarely used lithography. They also differ from other illustrations in their modern dress and decor.
Manet. 'Le Corbeau'. Lithographs (from pen and ink), 1875.

Fig. 22   Frontispiece.
Fig. 23   Ex-libris.
Fig. 24   'Une fois, par un minuit lugubre, tandis que je m'appentissais, faible et fatigué, sur maint curieux et bizarre volume de savoir oublié . . . Soudain se fit un heurt . . .' (190).

Hyperbole! de ma mémoire
Triomphalement, ne sais tu
Te lever, aujourd'hui grimoire
Dans un livre de fer vêtu   ('Prose pour des Esseintes', 55)

La chair est triste hélas! et
J'ai lu tous les livres . . .   (Brise marine', 38)

Ce scandement n'était-il pas le bruit du progrès
de mon personnage . . .
Enfin ce n'est pas le ventre vélu d'un hôte
inférieur de moi . . .   ('Igitur' 438–9)

Fig. 25   Au large je poussais le volet, quand, avec
maint enjouement et agitation d'ailes,
entra un majestueux corbeau . . .   (191)

. . . l'heure se formule en cet écho, au seuil
des panneaux ouverts par son acte de la
Nuit . . .   ('Igitur' 436)

Il a ployé son aile indubitable en moi   ('Quand l'ombre menaça' 67)

Fig. 26   . . . je roulais soudain un siège à coussins en
face de l'oiseau, et du buste, et de la porte . . .
je me pris a enchaîner songerie à songerie, . . .   (192)

Fig. 27   Ne laisse pas une plume noire, ci comme gage du
mensonge qu'a proféré ton âme . . . ôte ton bec de
mon coeur . . . Et mon âme, de cette ombre qui gît
flottante à terre, ne s'élèvera – jamais plus!   (193)

Some of the pen drawings Manet drafted for Mallarmé's planned illustrated edition of his prose translation of Poe's poems. They were published in 1888 with only a portrait of Poe and a 'fleuron' by Manet. (*Les Poèmes d'Edgar Poe*, Bruxelles, Deman, 1888) Mallarmé mentioned eight pictures by Manet related to Poe in a letter in May 1881. Together with the five for 'The Raven', these three would make up the eight. (*Correspondance* vol. 2, 222)
Dedicated: 'À la mémoire d'Edouard Manet ces feuillets que nous lûmes ensemble. S.M.' See Mallarmé, *Œuvres*, 1521 passim.

Fig. 28   Manet. *Annabel Lee*.
Fig. 29   Manet. *La Dormeuse*. Bibliothèque Nationale.
Fig. 30   Manet. *La Cité en la Mer*.
Fig. 31   Manet. *Le Vieux Musicien*. Oil. 1862. Washington, National Gallery.
Fig. 32   Redon, *À l'horizon l'ange des Certitudes, et dans un ciel sombre, un regard intérrogateur*. Lithograph. 1882. No. 4 of six in an album. *À Edgar Poe*.
Fig. 33   Gauguin. *D'où venons-nous, que sommes-nous, où allons-nous*. Oil. 1897. Museum of Fine Arts,

Boston. 'J'y mis là avant de mourir toute mon énergie ... la vie en surgit ...' (See Wildenstein, *Gauguin. Catalogue* 232f.) Gauguin painted it without premeditation as a final statement, convinced he was going to die. The letter quoted above also contains a commentary on his use of colour as musical chords.

Fig. 34   Manet. *Un Bar aux Folies Bergères.* Oil. 1882. Courtauld Institute Galleries, London (Courtauld Collection).

Fig. 35   Whistler, *Symphony in White No. 1: The White Girl.* 1862. Washington, National Gallery. A great success at the Salon des Refusés of 1863 (at which Manet's *Un Déjeuner sur l'Herbe* was exhibited.) (Sutton 'Nocturne', 198).

> C'est le portrait d'un spirite, d'un médium. La figure, L'attitude, la physionomie, la couleur sont étranges. C'est tout à la fois simple et fantastique.
>
> (J. K. Huysmans, *Certains*, 64)

Fig. 36   Whistler, *Symphony in White No. 2: The Little White Girl,* 1864. Tate Gallery.

> '... étrange, mystérieux, distingué, à la façon de Velasquez et d'Edgar Poe'. Gustav Geffroy in 1901, (quoted by Sutton, 'Nocturne' 185)

Fig. 37   Whistler, *Symphony in White No. 3.* 1865/7. The Barber Institute of Fine Arts, the University of Birmingham.

> Whistler sketched this in letter to Fantin-Latour and Degas copied it (Sutton 'Nocturne', 188).

Fig. 38   Manet. Frontispiece to *Collection de Huit Eaux-Fortes.* 1862. Bibliothèque Nationale.

> J'ai troué dans le mur de toile une fenêtre!   Mallarmé *Le Pitre Châtié*, 31

Fig. 39   Manet. *Portrait of Berthe Morisot.* Frontispiece for the catalogue of her posthumous exhibition, for which Mallarmé wrote the preface.

Fig. 40   Morisot, *Jeune Fille cueillant des Oranges.* Oil. 1889. Mallarmé owned this painting, now in a private collection in the U.S.A.

The following nine are from the album *Les Origines* by Redon. Lithographs. 1883.

Fig. 41   Cover.
Fig. 42   *Quand s'éveillait la vie au fond de la matière obscure.*
Fig. 43   *Il y eût peut-être une vision première essayée dans la fleur.*
Fig. 44   *Le polype difforme flottait sur les rivages, sorte de Cyclope souriant et hideux.*
Fig. 45   *La Sirène sortait des flots vêtue de dards.*
Fig. 46   *Le Satyre au cynique sourire.*
Fig. 47   *Il y eût des luttes et de vaines victoires.*
Fig. 48   *L'aile impuissante n'élèvera point la bête en ces noirs espaces.*
Fig. 49   *Et l'homme parut, interrogeant le sol d'où il sort et qui l'attire, il se fraya la voie vers de sombres clartés.*

> (See Sandström *Le monde imaginaire* and Viola 'Redon, Darwin, and the ascent of man', for accounts of this series as Darwinian, and in the wider context of eighteenth-century evolutionary theories)

Fig. 50   Puvis de Chavannes. *L'Espérance.* Oil. c.1871. Louvre.

> *L'Espérance* is a more personal expression of feeling after the end of the Franco-Prussian War. Though Puvis denied anything other than a 'visual' mode of signification, Gauguin repeatedly explored his texts and compared them with Mallarmé in his own experimentation with articulating ideas. He took a copy of *L'Espérance* and of Manet's *Olympia* to Tahiti. The frieze-like structure of *L'Été* is reflected in his *D'où venons-nous, que sommes-nous, où allons-nous* and that of several others in other paintings. For his writing on Puvis, see Wildenstein, *Gauguin. Catalogue.*

Fig. 51   Redon. *Le Masque de la Mort Rouge.* Charcoal. 1883. Museum of Modern Art, New York.

> 'J'étais l'heure qui doit me rendre pur,' 'Igitur' (435). Inspired by Poe's tale 'The Masque of the Red Death.' In 'Igitur' the ticking of the clock, Igitur's heartbeat and the beating of wings are overlaid, signifying his attempts to escape the constraints of time and history: 'ce

n'était pas quelque doute dernier de soi, qui remuait ses ailes par hasard en passant, mais le frottement familier et continu d'un âge supérieur' (437).

        plume solitaire éperdue

        sauf

              que la rencontre ou l'effleure une toque de minuit   'Un Coup de Dés' (468–9)

Fig. 52   Redon. 'Sous l'aile d'ombre, l'être noir appliquait une active morsure.' From the series *Songes*, 1891. One of six plates. Compare Mallarmé's image:

        Quand l'ombre menaça de la fatale loi

        Tel vieux Rêve, désir et mal de mes vertèbres,

        Affligé de périr sous les plafonds funèbres

        Il a ployé son aile indubitable en moi

                                                                            (67)

Figs. 53–58. Series *Hommage à Goya*. 1885.

Fig. 53   Redon. *Dans mon Rêve, je vis au ciel un visage de mystère.* 6 plates.

        See text for Mallarmé's comments on this plate. Redon sent him the series as a gift.

Fig. 54   Redon. *La fleur du marécage, une tête humaine et triste.*

        Mallarmé wrote of this plate, 'La tête de Rêve, cette fleur du marécage, illumine d'une clarté qu'elle connaît seule et qui ne sera pas dite, tout le tragique falot de l'existence ordinaire.' Compare with fig. 54 of *Les Origines*, and other severed head-flowers which it echoes. Redon studied botany under Clavaud, from whom he would have learnt about the marsh plant-animal which fertilised itself by releasing sperm which swam up to the corolla.

        C'est sur un cou qui raide émerge

        D'une fraise empesée idem

        Une face imberbe au cold-cream

        Un air d'hydrocéphale asperge.

        Les yeux sont noyés de l'opium

        De l'indulgence universelle

        La bouche clownesque ensorcèle

        Comme un singulier geranium.

        Laforgue, 'Pierrot', 1885.

Fig. 55   Redon. *Un fou dans un morne paysage.* Mallarmé wrote of this plate, 'Une sympathie bien mystérieuse vous a fait portraiturer dans ce délicieux hermite fou le pauvre petit homme que au fond de mon être j'aimerais être.'

Fig. 56   Redon. *Il y eût aussi des êtres embryonnaires.* Mallarmé wrote of this, 'Et quelle synthèse cruellement abrégée, sans étiolement là, mais presque satisfaite de la face intérieure de beaucoup, dans la planche IV.' This relays to foetal images, such as fig. 44 of *Les Origines* and Laforgue's 'Complainte de Foetus du poete' and Mallarmé's 'Don du Poème'.

Fig. 57   *Un étrange jongleur.* Mallarmé admired this the most after fig. 54: 'Mon autre préféré est, dans le même ordre de songes salomoniques, cet "étrange jongleur" à l'esprit devasté par la merveille au sens profond qu'il accomplit, et si souffrant dans le triomphe de son savant résultat.' Together they are interpreted as foreboding and triumph, as in 'Quand l'ombre menaça'.

Fig. 58   Redon. *Au réveil, j'aperçus la Déesse de l'Intelligible au profil sévère et dur.* Mallarmé wrote of this, the last plate, 'L'étude de femme, que vous appelez si justement la Déesse de l'Intelligible, nous sort à regret du cauchemar.' Intelligibility is not the aim of the experience, and there is a refusal or closing off in this expressionless face.

Fig. 59–61   These lithographs are Redon's illustrations for 'Un Coup de Dés' 1898. The dimensions are: figs. 59 and 60, 11 × 14 ins; fig. 61, 7¼ × 9 ins. They are untitled.

Fig. 62   Redon. *L'Intelligence fût à moi! Je devins le Buddha.* From the series *La Tentation de Saint Antoine* (third series) 1896, no. 12.

Fig. 63   Redon. *Et il avait dans sa main droite sept étoiles et de sa bouche sortait une epée aigüe à deux tranchants.* From the series *L'Apocalypse de Saint Jean.* 1899. Twelve plates plus cover. As with the series on Saint Anthony, the captions are all quotations from the written text, in this case the Bible.

Fig. 64   Redon. *C'est une tête de mort avec une couronne de roses. Elle domine une torse de femme d'une blancheur nacrée.* 1888. From the series *La Tentation de Saint Antoine,* no. 1. Ten plates plus cover. There were three in total including *À Gustave Flaubert* (1889). The third Saint Antoine was done in 1896.

Fig. 65   Redon. *La Mort: mon ironie dépasse tous les autres!* 1889, from the series *À Gustave Flaubert.* Six plates.

Fig. 66   Redon. Frontispiece for *Le Mouvement Idéaliste en Peinture* by Mellerio, 1896.

Fig. 67   Redon. *Mes baisers ont le gout d'un fruit qui se fondrait dans ton coeur . . . Tu me dédaignes! Adieu.* From the series *La Tentation de Saint Antoine* (third series). 1896, no. 4.
          Relay to the helmeted woman of 'Victorieusement fui' and to 'Hérodiade', 'Métaux qui donnez à ma jeune chevelure . . .' (47).

Fig. 68   Knopff. 'A la nue accablante tue . . .' 1895. Published in *Pan* no. 1, Berlin, with this facsimile of the poem in Mallarmé's handwriting. See *Documents Mallarmé,* vol. 2.

Fig. 69   Toorop. *The Three Brides.* Charcoal and coloured pencil. 1893.

Fig. 70   Redon. *Des Esseintes.* 1882. Frontispiece for *A Rebours* by J.-K. Huysmans. The atrophied body and the shadow make the head appear too large and virtually sever it from the body.

Fig. 71   Manet. *Olympia.* Oil. 1863. Louvre. A great deal has been written about this painting ever since it first appeared at the Salon des Refusés in 1864. Reference is made to it in most books on Manet, and a list may be found in Reff's *Olympia.* Apart from its technical innovations, two principal themes are centred on it; its derivation from Titian etc. and its signification as an image of contemporary women. Mallarmé described it as Baudelairean in its 'intellectual perversity', 'showing to the public for the first time the non-traditional, unconventional nude' (71). He thought it uneasily composed after 'the old masters of the north and south'. 'Captivating and repulsive, eccentric and new, such types as he gave us were needed . . .' ('The Impressionists and Edouard Manet', 71.)

Fig. 72   Manet. *Portrait of Jeanne Duval.* Oil. c.1862. Museum of Fine Arts. Budapest. Jeanne Duval was Baudelaire's Black mistress, and he dedicated several poems to her.

Fig. 73   Manet. *Le Repos.* Oil. c.1869. Rhode Island School of Art, Providence. One of several portraits by Manet of Berthe Morisot. After *Le Linge* perhaps one of Mallarmé's favourite paintings of women: 'exhaling all the lassitude of summertime . . . the jalousies of her room are almost closed, the dreamer's face is dim with shadow, but a vague, deadened daylight suffuses her figure and her muslin dress. This work is altogether exceptional and sympathetic.' In the planned edition of illustrated prose-poems, *Pages,* Morisot was to contribute an illustration for 'Le Nénuphar Blanc'. 'La chère ombre enfouie en de la batiste et les dentelles d'une jupe affluant sur le sol comme pour circonvenir du talon à l'orteil, dans une flottaison . . .' (285).

Fig. 74   Whistler. *Studies of Loie Fuller dancing.* Lithograph, n.d. Hunterian Art Gallery, University of Glasgow, Birnie Philips Bequest.
          Mallarmé wrote two articles on the dance, the second of which was about the American dancer. She used swirls of fabric held out on sticks and illuminated with electric light and radium, seeking a new form of dance on similar principles to those of Isadora Duncan and her return to Greek dance. Mallarmé described it as 'une ivresse d'art, et, simultanément, un accomplissement industriel. . . . le sortilège qu'opère la Loie Fuller, par instinct, avec l'exagération, les retraits de jupe ou d'aile, instituant un lieu.' (309) Whistler's copy of *La Revue Indépendante,* in which this appeared, has a sketch of a dancer on the back.

Fig. 75   *Hari and Vishnou.* From Kreuzer's *Hindu Gods,* known to Redon and Flaubert. (See Seznec *Nouvelles études.*)

Fig. 76   *Bhavani* or *Ganga.* From Kreuzer.

Fig. 77   Kupka. *The beginning of life.* c.1900. Kupka's *The Soul of the Lotus*, 1898, relays to these images and the legend.

Fig. 78   Gauguin. Sketch from *Noa Noa*. Imaginative journal of his voyage to Tahiti, transcribed by Charles Morice, 1893. Published 1901.

NOTES

1. Introduction

1 This also applies to 'unitary semiotic functions' by which I mean both simple signs in which only one trope (metaphor, abstract figure etc.) is used and the purely visual or aural. All signs are either visual or aural. See especially chapter 3. For further definitions see Jakobson *Selected Writings*, vol. II, 1971.

2 By 'transmutative operations' I mean the workings of signs which transgress the divide between the visual and the aural.

3 By 'intertextual' I mean concerning more than one text between which there may or may not be a factual relation. This includes visual and written or spoken texts.

4 By 'icon' I mean sign in which there is a shared quality between signifier and signified, especially an existential relation as in the 'index'. (See Jakobson *Selected Writings*, II, 700.) Icons are prevalent in purely spatial, visual signs. They do not assert or propose.

5 By 'symbol' I mean a sign which is associated with the represented object by a conventional rule. It denotes a kind of thing and has a general meaning. It cannot either indicate or be a single thing. Symbols are prevalent in temporal, auditory signs.

6 Page numbers in brackets refer to Mallarmé *Œuvres Complètes*, Gallimard, 1945, and in English, to his essay 'The Impressionists and Edouard Manet', which has only survived in the translation which Mallarmé approved, published in *Documents Mallarmé*, Nizet, 1968. (Text reproduced at the beginning of chapter 2.)

7 'Cézanne's Doubt' in *Essential Writings of Merleau-Ponty* (translated by Fisher), 1969.

8 By 'introversive' I mean a message which signifies itself, as in music. Introversive signs are non-representational and have little conceptual content. They have strong emotive connotations, however.

9 I am indebted to a wide variety of theoretical work; perhaps most immediately to Lacan, Kristéva, Ehrenzweig, Jakobson and Barthes. I am aware of the difficulties of combining several sources in this way, and of the limitations of Freud and Lacan in analysing texts, especially from a feminist standpoint.

10 By 'code' I mean the overall sign-system into which the specific message inserts. 'Code' and 'message' correspond to Saussure's 'langue' and 'parole'.

11 By 'cathexes' I mean the attachment of psychic energies to ideas or objects. See Laplanche and Pontalis *The Language of Psycho-Analysis* for this and all following definitions of Freudian terminology. Also Freud *Beyond the Pleasure Principle*, in *Standard Edition*, vol. 18, 236, 273; and on hysteria, e.g. vol. 1.

12 By 'scopic' I mean basically initiated by sight and with an awareness of separateness. This is simpler

and more restricted than Lacan's use. See Chapters 6 and 7 of *Les Quatre Concepts fondamentaux de la Psychanalyse*.
13 Mulford, *Red Letters*, no. 9, 40.

2. A new problematic of the imaginary

1 'M. Robinson a été charmant de tout point; et, à part quelques contre-sens faciles à redresser ... son excellente traduction fait honneur à ma prose, et rend ce travail passable.' (*Correspondance*, II, 130).
2 Barthélme 'Les Impressionistes'. The Pléiade edition of Mallarmé's *Œuvres* only has a note on it, while it contains the complete text of 'Le Jury de Peinture pour 1874 et M. Manet'. It was reprinted in *Documents Mallarmé*, vol 1 (1968).
3 See Harris 'Edouard Manet as illustrator', Bowness 'Manet and Mallarmé', Hanson *Manet and the Modern Tradition*.
4 *Des Gens du Monde à la Fenêtre* is *Le Balcon*. The two *Canotiers* are *En Bateau* and *Argenteuil*. I have not identified *Un Coin de Table*.
5 *Rêverie* is *Le Repos*.
6 By 'phoneme' I mean the minimum formal unit in language. It has no meaning in itself though it participates in signification.
7 See especially Hanson *Manet and the Modern Tradition*; Ives *The Great Wave*; etc.
8 See Jakobson and Waugh, *The Sound-shape of Language*.
9 See Ehrenzweig, *The Hidden Order of Art*, 35 and also 81 (on action painting and fragmentation).
10 By 'structural transposition' I mean the transfer of the *mode* of signification from one semiotic system to another.
11 By 'metonym' I mean a trope expressing an external relation of contiguity and remoteness. It is predominant in realism. It is opposed to 'metaphor' which expresses an internal relation of similarity and contrast. It is predominant in symbolism.
12 See Barthes, *Image, Music, Text* (translated by Heath), 17.
13 E. Zola was first to write in defence of Manet. See Zola *Le bon Combat*. He wrote more but to no greater effect than Mallarmé. Eventually he and Manet disagreed.
14 Proust, *Edouard Manet*.
15 Duret, *Les Peintres Impressionistes*.
16 See Fried, 'Manet's sources'.
17 Barthes, *Le Degré Zéro de l'Écriture*, 45.
18 Francastel, *La Réalité Figurative*.
19 By 'metalanguage' I mean language used to discuss language. See also Chapter 3 notes 1–3.
20 Valéry, *Écrits sur L'Art* 1960, 146.
21 Laforgue, *Mélanges*, 138.
22 ibid.
23 By 'entropic' I mean having an innate tendency towards repose, neutrality or equilibrium. This involves a levelling of the difference between internal and external, projection and retention. See Ehrenzweig, *The Hidden Order of Art*, 232 etc. and Jackson, *Fantasy*.
24 Kristeva, *La Révolution du Langage poétique*, 424–5.

3. Self sign world

1 "ces parages" – I read this as an interlingual pun on 'separate', though, of course, 'séparage' does not exist in French. Given Mallarmé's knowledge of English, other instances encourage exploration of this interlingual area as a source of extended meaning – 'prestige': 'the artificial prestige cast by candelabra or footlights' ('The Impressionists and Edouard Manet' 74), 'prestiges situés à ce point de l'ouïe et presque de la vision abstraite' (649); 'plume', see below p. 00; and Mallarmé adopted the *nom de plume* L. S. Price when he reported on the National Exhibition in London in 1871. In French this would be L. S. Prix, or 'L'Esprit'. (Another *nom de plume*: Ix 'La Dernière Mode'. Cf 'Ses purs ongles'.)

2 By an 'autonymous mode' I mean a message referring to the code. See below notes 3 and 4.

3 Barthes, *Mythologies*, 109f.

4 There are four duplex types of semiosis which both utilise and refer to the message or code as just listed. See Jakobson *Selected Writings* II, 131 ff. By 'shifter' I mean an indexical symbol which combines an existential with a conventional relation. It can only be defined with reference to the message.

5 See Foucault *Les mots et les choses*.

6 On colour and emotive signification see Kristeva *Polylogue*, 383–408. Also Ehrenzweig, *The Hidden Order of Art* 126 etc.

7 This painting inspired Swinburne's poem 'Before the Mirror'. It was re-interpreted by Montesquieu (the model for Des Esseintes and a friend of Mallarmé and Whistler) in his poem 'White Rose' (title in English).

8 By 'ostension' I mean the semiotic display of objects, including bodies. The definition in the text, as the type of semiosis of actors in the theatre, is a specific example.

9 See also my discussion of zero signification, p. oo.

10 By 'Projection' I mean the transferral of qualities, feelings or perceptions from the self to other persons or things. See Laplanche and Pontalis, *The Language of Psycho-Analysis*, 349.

11 Simultaneous synthesis is discussed later in this chapter. See also p. oo, discussion of 'pendentif' image.

12 Differentiated/dedifferentiated perception, like syncretic vision, accommodates incompatible forms with a broader focus than conscious perception; its precision remains unconscious. See also note 20.

13 Quoted in Mellerio 1913, 23.

14 By 'relay' I mean the setting up of contiguous relations which advance the message. The total message is realised at a higher level. Barthes pairs this with 'anchor', the function of holding/directing meaning, and, to some extent, limiting it. See Barthes, *Image, Music, Text*, p. 41. Cf. syntagm and paradigm, note 16.

15 'Confidences d'artiste', 29.

16 By 'syntagm' I mean elementary combinations. The opposing operation is the paradigm, based on selection. These are the basic linguistic operations. See Jakobson *Selected Writings* II, 525 etc.

17 *Polylogue*, 408.

18 See Freud, *The Interpretation of Dreams*, *Standard Edition* vol. 4, 120–133 and *Jokes and their relation to the Unconscious*, vol. 8, 215–258.

19 See Freud, *Jokes and their relation to the Unconscious*, *Standard Edition* vol. 8.

20 By 'primary process' I mean not an earlier or irrational level of thought, but a new matrix, an undifferentiated structure facilitating innovation of concepts and images. See Ehrenzweig *The Hidden Order of Art* 272 ff.

21 By 'affect' I mean the 'qualitative expression of the quantity of instinctual energy'. Laplanche and Pontalis *The Language of Psycho-Analysis*, 13.

22 Freud, *Standard Edition* vol. 14, 337 ff. and vol. 18, 273.

23 Freud, *Psychoanalytic Notes on an autobiographical case of Paranoia*, *Standard Edition* vol. 12, 3–80.

24 Eliot, T. S., 'Dante' in *Selected Essays*, 243.

25 *Paradiso*, Canto XV.

26 See Freud, *Standard Edition* vol. 19, 227f. The 'mystic writing pad' was a mechanical device which transferred messages written on the surface on to an internal layer, thus retaining an apparently erased message.

27 Cf passage on projection, which is a related function, though not the same. Many of Redon's late pastels show figures emanating light, like an inversion of fig. 69 in which the figure is born out of its shell. Le Maître in 'Un Coup de Dés' relates similarly to the hull of the boat and the furrowed waves. See chapter 5.

28 Valéry, *Écrits sur L'Art* 1960, 146.

29 'Confidences d'Artiste', 29.

30 Like dedifferentiated vision, this is uncoded perception. See notes 12 and 20.
31 See Ehrenzweig *The Hidden Order of Art* and fantasies of the self-creating child, 204–224; and Freud on bisexuality and hysteria *Standard Edition*, vol. 9.
32 See Sandström *Le monde imaginaire* and Viola 'Redon, Darwin, and the ascent of Man'.
33 In his notes to Bernard's articles on his work, Redon wrote 'Je ne suis point Darwiniste, car je ne fais pas de science'. See Rewald, 'Quelques notes et documents'.
34 'Le Monstre' in *Certains*.
35 'Confidences d'Artiste' 30.
36 ibid.
37 Kristeva, Σημειωτική, p. 6.
38 See below, comparing 'Quand l'ombre menaça' with fig. 68.
39 See Wildenstein *Gauguin. Catalogue*.
40 *Correspondance*, 1, 277–79. The poem was intended to be illustrated with an etching for inclusion in Philippe Burty's *Sonnets et Eaux-Fortes*.
41 Jakobson and Waugh, *The Sound-Shape of Language*.
42 ibid.
43 ibid., *Signe Zéro*, 211–22.
44 ibid., 289–306. Jakobson's writing on aphasia, especially the two intermediate types sets out the framework in terms of encoding and decoding disorders and relates them to language acquisition.
45 Lacan, *Les Quatre Concepts*.
46 See Freud *Standard Edition* vol. 8, 220.
47 ibid.
48 See Signac, *D'Eugène Delacroix au Néo-Impressionisme* and Rewald, *Post Impressionism*. Contrast Gauguin in Wildenstein *Gauguin. Catalogue* and Rewald, *Gauguin*.
49 By 'synecdochic' I mean the use of a detail to initiate a series of contiguous relationships.
50 See Freud on *Distortion in Dreams and Jokes*, in *Standard Edition*, vol. 8, 159–180, and in *Hysteria* in *Standard Edition* vol, 9, 157f.
51 By 'graphemic' I mean signifying patterns of writing.
52 Freud *Standard Edition* vol. 8 136–7.
53 ibid., 138, n. 1.
54 ibid., 220.
55 ibid., 189–90. Baudelaire's essay on caricature *De l'Essence du Rire* concerns this kind of comic of movement, described in terms of pantomime.
56 ibid., 191.

4. 'Un Coup de Dés' as illustrated poem

1 See Bacou *Odilon Redon* and Berger *Odilon Redon*.
2 See Bacou and Redon eds., *Lettres à Redon* and Mallarmé's *Correspondance*, vol. 2, 279 passim.
3 See Bacou *Odilon Redon*, and Finke ed., *French Nineteenth Century Painting*.
4 ibid.
5 Barthes, *Gramma*, VII, 6.
6 ibid.
7 Valéry, *Écrits diverses*, 20.

5. Gender-in-Signification

1 Lacan, in *Le Séminaire*, for example. 'De la Jouissance' moves in and out of psychoanalytic discourse across the female body and Bellini's image of it in Saint Thérèse. 'C'est ce que le discours analytique démontre, en ceci que, pour un de ces êtres comme sexués, pour l'homme en tant qu'il est pour vu de l'organe dit phallique – j'ai dit dit – le sexe corporel, le sexe de la femme – j'ai dit de la femme, alors que, justement il n'y a pas *la* femme, la femme n'est *pas toute* – le sexe de la femme ne lui dit rien, si ce n'est pas par l'intermédiaire du corps.' (13)

2 *Correspondance* I, 246.
3 Fuller, *Art and Psychoanalysis* returns to it.
4 Huysmans, *Certains*, for example, or *The Sacred and Profane in Symbolist Art* (exhibition catalogue) Toronto 1969.
5 Sollers, *Logiques*, 15.
6 ibid., 30.
7 ibid., 31.
8 ibid., 31.
9 Freud, *The Theme of the Three Caskets Standard Edition*, vol. 12, 91.
10 Sollers, *Logiques*, 31.
11 Derrida, *Speech and Phenomena*.
12 Active/Passive: see Laplanche and Pontalis *The Language of Psycho-Analysis*, 8–9.

6. Concluding note

1 Reprinted in translation in *New French Feminisms*, 1981, 97.
2 T. J. Clark's reading of *Olympia*, 'Manet's "Olympia" in 1865' (*Screen*, vol. 21, no. 1, 1980, 18–41) initiated an interesting dialogue between himself and Peter Wollen on this question of 'modernism' and coherence. See also *Screen* vol. 21, nos. 2 and 3.

BIBLIOGRAPHY

Anderson, R., 'Hindu Myths in Mallarmé: *Un Coup de Dés*', *Comparative Literature*, XIX (1967) 28–35.

Angoulvent, M., *Berthe Morisot*, Edns. Albert Morancé, 1933.

Aurier, G., *Œuvres Posthumes*, Mercure de France, 1893.

Aurier, G. A., 'Le Symbolisme en peinture: Paul Gauguin', *Mercure de France* (mars, 1891) 155–65.

Austin, L. J., 'Mallarmé on music and Letters', *Bull. John Rylands Lib. Manchester* XLII, i (Sept. 1959).

Austin, L. J., 'Mallarmé Critique d'Art', in *The Artist and Writer in France*, F. Haskell, A. Levi, and R. Shackleton (eds.) Oxford, Clarendon Press, 1974.

Bacou, R., *Odilon Redon*, 2 vols. Geneva, Cailler, 1956.

Bacou R., and Redon, A., (eds.) *Lettres à Redon*, Corti, 1960.

Barbier, C. P., (ed.) *Mallarmé. Recueil de 'Nursery Rhymes'*, Gallimard, 1965.

Barbier, C. P., (ed.) *Correspondance Mallarmé-Whistler* Nizet, 1964.

Barbier, C. P., (ed.) *Documents Mallarmé*, vols 1–16. Nizet, 1968–77.

Barthélme, M., 'Les Impressionistes et Edouard Manet', *N.R.F.*, (Aug. 1959) 232–57.

Barthes, R., *Mythologies*, Edns. du Seuil, 1957.

Barthes, R., *Elements of Semiology*, Cape, 1967.

Barthes, R., *L'Empire des Signes*, Geneva, Skira, 1970.

Barthes, R., *S/Z*, Edns. du Seuil, 1970.

Barthes, R., *Le Degré Zéro de l'Écriture*, Edns. du Seuil, 1972.

Barthes, R., (trans. Heath) *Image, Music, Text*, Fontana, 1977.

Barthes, R., 'Question de tempo – à Lucette Finas', *Gramma*, VII (1977) 5–7.

Bataille, G., and Wildenstein, G., *Berthe Morisot. Catalogue Raisonné*, Les Beaux-Arts, Paris 1961.

Berger, K., *Odilon Redon. Fantasy and Colour*, London and New York, 1965.

Blanchot, M., *L'Espace Littéraire*, Gallimard, 1955.

Boime, A., *The Academy and nineteenth century French Painting*, Phaidon, 1971.

Bowie, M., *Mallarmé and the art of being difficult*, Cambridge, C.U.P., 1978.

Bowness, A., 'Manet and Mallarmé', *Bull. Philadelphia Museum of Art*, LXII, No. 293 (April–June, 1967), 212–22.

Bowness, A., 'Poetry as Art Criticism: Mallarmé and Manet', *Bulletin Philadelphia Museum of Art*, No. 292 (1966).

Brookner, A., *The Genius of the Future: Studies in French Art Criticism*, Phaidon, 1971.

Burgin, V., 'Photography', *Screen*, vol. 21 no. 1 (Spring 1980) 43–80.

Butor, M., *Les Mots dans la Peinture*, Paris 1969.

Cazalis, H., *Henri Regnault, sa Vie, son Œuvre*, Lemerre, 1872.

Cixous, H., (trans. A. Kuhn) 'Castration or Decapitation?' *Signs* vol. 7 no. 1 (Autumn 1981), 41–56.

Clark, T. J., 'Manet's "Olympia" in 1865'. *Screen*, vol. 21 no. 1 (Spring 1980) 18–41.

Clark, T. J., *Image of the People*, Thames and Hudson, 1973.

Clark, T. J., *The Absolute Bourgeois*, Thames and Hudson, 1973.

Cohn, R. G., *Mallarmé's Masterwork*, The Hague, Mouton, 1966.

Courthion, P., (ed.) *Manet raconté par lui-même et par ses amis*, Geneva, Cailler, 1953.

Decaudin, M., 'Poésie impressioniste et poésie symboliste', *12e. Cahier de l'Assoc. des Études Français*, (1960), 133–42.

DeLeiris, A., *The Drawings of Edouard Manet*, Berkeley/L.A., U. Ca. Press. 1969.

Delevoy, L., *Symbolists and Symbolism*, Macmillan, 1978.

De Regnier, H., *Nos Rencontres*, Mercure de France, 1931.

De Regnier, H., *Proses Datées*, Mercure de France, 1925.

Derrida, J., *L'Écriture et la Différence*, Edns. du Seuil, 1967.

Derrida J., *La Dissémination*, Edns. du Seuil, 1972.

Derrida, J., *Speech and Phenomena*, Evanston, Northwestern, 1973.

Duret, T., 'Whistler et son œuvre', *Les Lettres et les Arts*, 3e. année, I (1888) 215–226.

Duret, T., *Les Peintres Impressionistes*, Heymann et Perois, 1878.

Ehrenzweig, A., *The Hidden Order of Art: a study in the psychology of artistic imagination*, Weidenfeld and Nicolson, 1957.

Ehrenzweig, A., *The Psychoanalysis of artistic vision and hearing*, Sheldon Press, 1975.

Eliot, T. S., *Selected Essays*, London, Faber, 1961.

Fenéon, F., 'Huysmans' *Certains*,' *Art et Critique*, No. 29 (14 dec., 1889).

Fenéon, F., 'Les Peintres Graveurs', *Le chat noir*, (25 avril, 1891).

Finke, U., (ed.) *French Nineteenth Century Painting and Literature*, Manchester U.P., 1972.

Foucault, M., *Les mots et les choses: une archéologie des sciences humaines*, Gallimard, 1966.

Fouchet, M. P., (ed.) *An Introduction with Letters and Writings by Gauguin*, 1975.

Fourreau, A., (trans. Wellington) *Berthe Morisot*, Bodley Head, 1925.

Fowlie, W., 'Mallarmé and the Painters of his Age' *Southern Review*, II (1966), 542–58.

Fraenkel, E., *Les Dessins trans-conscients de Mallarmé*, Nizet, 1960.

Francastel, P., *La Réalité Figurative: éléments structurels de l'art*, Gonthier, 1965.

Freud, S., (eds. Strachey J., et al) *Standard Edition of the Complete Psychological Works*, 24 vols. Hogarth, 1953–74.

Fried, M., 'Manet's Sources' *Art Forum*, 1969.

Fuller, P., *Art and Psychoanalysis*, Writers and Readers, 1981.

Garbaty, T. J., 'The French Coterie of *The Savoy*', *P.M.L.A.*, 1960.

Garnier, P., *Spatialisme et Poésie Concrète*, Gallimard, 1968.

Gauguin, P., 'Exposition de la libre esthétique' *Essais d'Art Libre*, Paris 1894, 30–32.

Gauguin, P., *Avant et Après*, Edns. Cres et Cie, Paris, 1923.

Gauguin, P., Morice, C., (trans. Green, J.) *Noa Noa–Voyage to Tahiti*, Oxford, 1961.

Gautier, T., 'La République de l'Avenir', *Le Journal*, (juillet, 1848).

Gautier, T., *Les Beaux-Arts en Europe*, 1855.

Gombrich, E., and Kris, E., *Caricature*, King Penguin, 1940.

Hamilton, A., *Manet and his Critics*, Newhaven/Yale, 1954.

Hanson, A. C., *Manet and the Modern Tradition*, New Haven/London, Yale U.P. 1977.

Harris, J. C., *Edouard Manet, Graphic Works, A definitive Catalog Raisonné*, New York, 1970.

Harris, J. C., 'Edouard Manet as illustrator', *Bull. Philadelphia Museum of Art*, LXII, No. 293 (April–June 1967) 223–35.

Harris, J. C., 'A little-known essay on Manet by S. Mallarmé', *The Art Bulletin*, XLVI, no. 4 (Dec. 1964) 559–63.

Heath, S., 'Difference', *Screen* (Autumn 1978), 51–112.

Henry, C., 'Introduction à l'esthétique scientifique', *Revue Contemporaine*, (25 août 1885).

Hobbs, R., *Odilon Redon*, Studio Vista, 1977.

Huyghe, R., *Le Carnet de Paul Gauguin*, Editart, 1952.

Huysmans, J.-K., *L'Art Moderne*, Charpentier, 1883.

Huysmans, J.-K., *À Rebours*, Paris, 1884.

Huysmans, J.-K., *Certains*, Tresse et Stock, 1889.

Irigaray, L., *Ce sexe qui n'en est pas un*, Edns. du Minuit, 1977.

Ives, C., *The Great Wave: The Influence of Japanese Woodcuts on French Prints*, Boston/New York, N.Y. Graphic Society/Metropolitan Museum of Art, 1971.

Jackson, R., *Fantasy. The Literature of Subversion*, New Accents, Methuen, 1981.

Jakobson, R., *Selected Writings*, (5 vols.) Mouton, The Hague, 1962–79.

Jakobson, R., and Waugh, L., *The Sound-Shape of Language*, Brighton, Harvester, 1979.

Jakobson, R., (and others) 'Language and Synaestnesia', in *Word*, 1949, 224–33.

Jardine, A., 'Introduction to Julia Kristeva's 'Women's Time', *Signs*, vol. 7 no. 1 (Autumn 1981) 5–12.

Johnson, B., *Défigurations du Langage Poétique*, Flammarion, 1980.

Jamot, P., and Wildenstein, G., *Catalogue Critique de l'oeuvre de Manet*, 2 vols. 1932.

Jullian, P., *Esthètes et Magiciens*, Perrin, 1969.

Jullian, P., *The Symbolists*, Phaidon, 1973.

Kahnweiler, D. H., 'Mallarmé et la peinture' *Les Lettres*, no. speciale sur Mallarmé (1948), 63–8.

Kaplan, C., et. al., 'Papers on Patriarchy', unpublished conference papers.

Kravis, J., *The Prose of Mallarmé: Evolution of a Literary Language*, California, 1976.

Kris, E., *Psychoanalytic Explorations in Art*, New York, International U.P. 1952.

Kristeva, J., Σημειωτική *Recherches pour un Semanalyse*, Edns. du Seuil, 1969.

Kristeva, J., *La Révolution du Langage Poétique*, Edns. du Seuil, Coll. Tel Quel, 1974.

Kristeva, J., *Polylogue*, Edns. du Seuil, 1977.

Kristeva, J., (trans. Gora, Jardine and Roudiez) *Desire in Language: a semiotic approach to Art*, Oxford, Blackwell, 1981.

Lacan, J., *Le Séminaire de Jacques Lacan. Livre xx. (1972–1973)*, Paris, Edns. du Seuil, 1975.

Lacan, J., *Écrits*, 2 vols., Coll. Points, Seuil, 1966–71.

Lacan, J., *Les Quatres Concepts fondamentaux de la Psychanalyse*, Edns. du Seuil, 1973.

Laforgue, J., *Œuvres Complètes*, Mercure de France, 1965.

Laforgue, J., *Mélanges Posthumes*, Mercure de France, 1903.

Laplanche, J., and Pontalis, J-B., *The Language of Psycho-Analysis*, Hogarth, 1973.

Lefèvre-Roujon, L., 'Oscar Wilde, Whistler et Mallarmé' *Journal de Genève*, (22–3 avril, 1951).

Lefèvre-Roujon, L., 'Mallarmé et les Peintres' *Journal de Genève*, (9–10 Sept. 1951).

Lehmann, A. G., 'Un Aspect de la critique symboliste. Signification et ambiguité dans les beaux-arts', *12e. Cahier de l'Association des Études Français*, (1960) 161–74.

Lévi-Strauss, C., *Tristes Tropiques*, Plon, 1955.

Lévi-Strauss, C., *Myth and Meaning*, Routledge and Kegan Paul, 1978.

Levy, M., *Whistler Lithographs*, Jupiter, 1975.

Lucie-Smith, E., *Symbolist Art*, Thames and Hudson, 1972.

Mackintosh, A., *Symbolism and Art Nouveau*, Thames and Hudson, 1975.

McIntosh, C., *Eliphas Levi and the French Occult Revival*, Rider, 1972.

Malingue, M., (ed.) *Lettres de Gauguin à sa femme et à ses amis*, Paris, 2nd augmented edn., 1949.

Mallarmé, S., *Oeuvres Complètes*, Paris, Gallimard, 1945.

Manet, E., *Manet raconté par lui-même et par ses amis*, Geneva, Cailler, 1953.

Marks, E., and de Courtivron, I., (eds.) *New French Feminisms*, Harvester, 1981.

Mauclair, C., 'Exposition O. Redon chez Durand Ruel'. *Mercure de France*, xi (mai, 1894) 94–5.

Mauner, G., *Manet, Peintre-Philosophe*, Pennsylvania State U.P., 1977.

Mauron, C., *Introduction à la Psychanalyse de Mallarmé*, La Baconnière, Neuchâtel, 1968.

Mauron, C., 'Mallarmé et le Tao' *Cahiers du Sud*, 246 (mai, 1942) 351–66.

Mellerio, A., *Le mouvement idéaliste en peinture*, Floury, 1896.

Mellerio, A., *Odilon Redon: oeuvre graphique complet*, The Hague, Artz and Du Bois, n.d. [1913]. Reissued New York, Da Capo, 1968.

Metz, C., *Essais Sémiotiques*, Klincksieck, 1977.

Michelet, H., *Le Peuple*, Marcel Didier, 1946.

Mitchell, J., *Psychoanalysis and Feminism*, Allen Lane, 1974.

Mitchell, J., and Rose, J., (eds.) *Jacques Lacan and the École Freudienne. Feminine Sexuality*, Macmillan, 1982.

Mondor, H., and Austin, L. J., (eds.) *Mallarmé Correspondance*, 4 vols. Vol. I, 1862–1871, published in 1959; vol. II, 1871–1885, published in 1965; vol. III, 1885–1889, published in 1968; vol. IV i, 1890–1891, published in 1973; vol. IV ii, Supplements to vols. I–III published in 1973. All volumes Paris, Gallimard.

Mondor, H., and Austin, L., *Les 'Gossips' de Mallarmé. 'Atheneum', 1875–76.* Gallimard, 1962.

Mondor, H., *Vie de Mallarmé*, Gallimard, 1941.

Mondor, H., *S. Mallarmé. Documents Iconographiques*, Geneva, Cailler, 1947.

Mulford, W., *Red letters*, No. 9 1981, 40.

Panofsky, E., *Meaning in the Visual Arts*, New York, Garden City, 1955.

Parker, R., and Pollock, G., *Old Mistresses: Women, Art and Ideology.* Routledge and Kegan Paul, 1981.

Pater, W., *Studies in the History of the Renaissance*, London, Macmillan, 1873.

Paxton, N., *The Development of Mallarmé's Prose Style*, Geneva, Droz, 1968.

Pennell, E. R. and J., *The Life of James McNeill Whistler*, 2 vols., Heinemann, 1908.

Poulet, G., *The Metamorphoses of the Circle*, Baltimore, Johns Hopkins, 1966.

Proust, A., *Edouard Manet: Souvenirs*, Paris, 1913.

Redon, O., et al., ed. C. Morice., 'Quelques opinions sur Paul Gauguin' *Mercure de France*, (1894) 428–30.

Redon, O., 'Confidences d'artiste' *La Vie*, (nov.–dec. 1912).

Redon, O., *Lettres 1878–1916*, (publiées par sa famille). 1923.

Redon, O., *A soi-même. Journal 1867–1915*, Corti, 1961.

Reff, T., 'Manet's sources: A Critical Evaluation' *Art Forum*, VIII, No. 1 (Sept. 1969) 40–48.

Reff, T., 'The symbolism of Manet's frontispiece etchings' *Burlington Magazine*, CIV (1962) 182–86.

Reff, T., *Manet: Olympia*, Allen Lane, 1976.

Rewald, J., *Gauguin*, Heinemann, 1949.

Rewald, J., 'Quelques notes et documents sur Odilon Redon', *Gazette des Beaux-Arts* (Nov. 1956).

Rewald, J., *Post Impressionism.* Secker and Warburg, 1978.

Richard, J. P., *L'Univers Imaginaire de Mallarmé.* Edns. du Seuil, 1962.

Richard, J. P., 'Feu rué, feu scintillé. Note sur Mallarmé, le fantasme et l'écriture', *Littérature*, No. 17 (fev. 1975) 84–104.

Richard, J. P., (ed.) *Pour un Tombeau d'Antatole*, Edns. du Seuil, 1961.

Roger Marx, C., 'Des Femmes Peintres et l'Impressionisme: Berthe Morisot', *Gazette des Beaux-Arts*, (dec. 1907).

Rookmaaker, H. R., *Gauguin and nineteenth-century Art Theory*, Amsterdam, Swets and Zeitlinger, 1972.

Rookmaaker, H. R., *Synthetist Art Theories*, Amsterdam, Swets and Zeitlinger, 1959.

Rossetti, W. M., 'Pre-Raphaelitism – its starting-point and its sequel' *Art Monthly Review*, No. 8 (Aug. 31, 1876).

Rouart-Valéry, A., 'Degas in the Circle of Paul Valéry', *Art News*, (Nov. 1960).

Rouart, D., (ed.) *Correspondance de Berthe Morisot*, Edns. Quatre Chemins, 1959.

Rouart, D., and Wildenstein, D., *Edouard Manet. Catalogue Raisonné*, 2 vols., La Bibliothèque des Arts, 1977.

Rougon, J., 'Whistler et Mallarmé (1888–98)' *Mercure de France*, (1 Dec. 1955) 631–60.

Sandblad, N., *E. Manet: 3 Studies in artistic conception*, Gleerup, Lund, 1954.

Sandström, S., *Le monde imaginaire d'Odilon Redon*, Lund, Berlingska, 1955.

Sartre, J. P., 'Mallarmé – Poetry and Suicide', in *From Existentialism to Marxism*, New Left Books, 1975.

Sartre, J. P., *L'imaginaire: psychologie phénoménologique de l'imagination*, Gallimard, 1940.

Selz, J., *Odilon Redon*, Lugano, Uffici, 1971.

Seznec, J. J., *Nouvelles Études sur 'La Tentation de Saint Antoine'*, Warburg Institute, 1949.
Seznec, J. J., *Literature and the Visual Arts in nineteenth century France*, University of Hull, 1963.
Seznec, J. J., 'Flaubert and the Graphic Arts', *Journal of Warburg and Courtauld Institutes*, VIII (1945) 175–90.
Shattuck, R., *The Banquet Years: The Arts in France 1885–1918*, Faber, 1969.
Signac, P., *D'Eugène Delacroix au Néo-Impressionisme*, Hermann, 1964.
Sollers, P., *Logiques*, Edns. du Seuil, Coll. Tel Quel, 1968.
Soulas, P., 'Mallarmé et la peinture de son temps', *Le Point*, No. speciale sur Mallarmé (fev.–avril, 1944).
Steinmetz, J. L., 'Mallarmé en Corps', *Littérature*, XVII (fev. 1975).
Stevens, W., *The Necessary Angel*, Faber, 1960.
Sutton, D., 'Nocturne: The Art of James McNeill Whistler', *Country Life*, 1963.
Symons, A., *Studies in the Seven arts*, Martin Secker, 1924.
Symons, A., 'A French Blake: Odilon Redon', *Art Review* (July, 1890) 206.
Tabarant, A., *Manet et ses œuvres*, Gallimard, 1947.
Thierry-Norbet, J., 'Mallarmé et Manet', *Le Monde Français*, VII, No. 23 (août, 1947) 331–34.
Thoré, T., *Salons de T. Thoré*, Librairie Internationale, 1868.
Valéry, P., *Écrits divers sur Stéphane Mallarmé*, Paris, Gallimard, 1950.
Valéry, P., *Écrits sur L'Art*, Paris, Gallimard, 1960.
Viola, J., 'Redon, Darwin and the ascent of Man', *Marsyas*, XI (1962–4) 42–57.
Whistler, J. McN., *The Gentle Art of Making Enemies*, 1st ed. 1890, Heinemann, 1953.
Wildenstein, G., *Gauguin, Catalogue*, Les Beaux-Arts (Edns. d'études et de documents) 1964.
Wind, E., *Pagan Mysteries in the Renaissance*, Faber, 1958.
Wollen, P., 'Manet: Modernism and Avant-Garde'. *Screen*, vol. 21, No. 2 (Summer 1980).
Woolley, G., 'Comments on Mallarmé's cubism and preciosity', *L'esprit créateur*, I, No. 3 (Fall 1961).
Zola, É., (eds. Picon, G., and Bouillon, J. P.) *Le bon Combat: (Écrits sur l'Art) De Courbet aux Impressionistes*, Hermann, Coll. Savoir, 1974.

Exhibition Catalogues

Odilon Redon, Paris, Oct. 1956–Jan. 1957.
O. Redon, G. Moreau, R. Bresdin, New York, 1961.
Manet, Degas, Morisot, Cassat, Baltimore, 1962.
Manet, Philadelphia, 1966.
The Sacred and Profane in Symbolist Art, Toronto, 1969.
From Realism to Symbolism. Whistler and his World, Columbia University and Philadelphia Museum of Art. March–May 1971.
French Symbolist Painters, Arts Council, 1972.
Impressionism, Royal Academy, London, 1974.
Gustave Courbet, Arts Council, 1978.
From Manet to Toulouse-Lautrec, British Museum, 1978.
Post-Impressionism, Royal Academy of Arts, 1979–80.
Abstraction: Towards a New Art, Tate Gallery, 1981.

INDEX

INDEX OF AUTHORS AND PROPER NAMES

Illustrations are shown by italic page numbers

For EU product safety concerns, contact us at Calle de José Abascal, 56–1°,
28003 Madrid, Spain or eugpsr@cambridge.org.

www.ingramcontent.com/pod-product-compliance
Ingram Content Group UK Ltd.
Pitfield, Milton Keynes, MK11 3LW, UK
UKHW030902150625
459647UK00021B/2674